Teaching Old Dogs New Tricks

Teaching Old Dogs New Tricks

*Driving Corporate Innovation Through Start-ups,
Spinoffs, and Venture Capital*

Tom Waters

BUSINESS EXPERT PRESS

Leader in applied, concise business books

Teaching Old Dogs New Tricks:
Driving Corporate Innovation Through Start-ups, Spinoffs, and Venture Capital

Cover design by Charlene Kronstedt

Interior design by Exeter Premedia Services Private Ltd., Chennai, India

First published in 2022 by
Business Expert Press, LLC
222 East 46th Street, New York, NY 10017
www.businessexpertpress.com

ISBN-13: 978-1-63742-340-0 (paperback)
ISBN-13: 978-1-63742-341-7 (e-book)

Business Expert Press Entrepreneurship and Small Business Management Collection

First edition: 2022

10 9 8 7 6 5 4 3 2 1

This book is dedicated to Rachael, Sarah, and Julian.
Be there for each other.
You reflect all that was ever good in me.

Description

This book will appeal to the multitude of corporate managers responsible for "innovation" when they have no idea how to make that happen. C-suite executives and boards of directors are increasingly looking for companies to reinvent themselves or risk being left behind.

Almost every big company in the United States requires their employees to assign their intellectual property rights to the firm. Anything the employee creates on company *dime and time* belongs to the employer. The problem is most of these contracts are not worth the paper they are printed on, because corporations rarely create anything from their employees' ideas.

It will allow companies to monetize employee's ideas in a manner that doesn't cost a fortune or create conflicts of interest within the ranks. Not every creative expression is going to result in tens of millions of dollars in revenue—but many will create licensing opportunities that are, at the very least, essentially free money for new product development.

Another cadre of readers will realize their innovation-rich futures are languishing in corporate purgatory. Should they quit and pitch their *million dollar idea* to another organization entirely (as outsiders), or can they take this book to their leaders and drive change, one manager at a time?

Keywords

3D print; 5G wireless; accelerator; Artificial Intelligence; autonomous; cloud computing; corporate venture capital; data analytics; disruption; dragonflies; drones; electric vehicles; incubator; joint research agreements; megatrends; network effects; Peter Drucker, ransomware; recording studio; sound city; start-up; strategy; supply chain; war

Contents

List of Figures

Disclaimer

Foreword

Peter Drucker, one of my favorite strategic thinkers, defines innovation as, *change that creates a new dimension of performance.*

When I discuss innovation, I'm not talking a corporation's *current* business practices. What I'm outlining herein is creating *new* products and services to ensure that a corporation will remain a going concern over the long term.

Many people use the words incubator and accelerator interchangeably and that's fine. Some consider corporate incubators and corporate venture capital to be the same. They're not, but that's ok too. They are at least looking for new opportunities and not simply doing things *the way we've always done them.*

This book is looking at over-the-horizon long-range vision and strategy. Not for the next fiscal quarter, but rather for the next quarter century. Everything happening today is simply shaping what will take place tomorrow. This is about finding and supporting the people shaping that tomorrow.

Start-ups are increasingly digitizing analog things. When was the last time you *unfolded* a map? It's probably been years. Why? Because digital maps are pervasive—not simply in the car but on your smartphone. This kind of change requires different kinds of thinking.

Maybe you're looking at new ways of doing old things. That physical map is one good example of this. Printed (foldable) electronics is another, the ability to make circuitry very small and able to fit into devices it couldn't previously. Or perhaps you're considering old things in new ways, like maybe 3D printing a golf putter, personalizing it for a specific individual's height, weight, and physical characteristics.

Large corporations often need help in this area, having become quite successful (and comfortable) in the old ways of doing things. That complacency gives a disruptive start-up all the ammunition they need to drive innovation to that waiting market.

Note that subtitle reads *Driving Corporate Innovation Through Start-ups, Spinoffs, and Venture Capital*—that means championing it. If that's not your intent you'll want to turn back now.

Introduction

Failure Is a Requirement, Not an Option

Quite a few years ago, I worked undercover on the Central Intelligence Agency's (CIA's) Economic and Trade Security team. Basically, I was the guy who showed up on a CEO's doorstep, flashed an ID with my false name, and said *I'm from the government and I'm here to help*. Yeah, *that* guy.

Unfortunately, I was always delivering *bad* news—frequently the case was that we'd discovered a foreign spy stealing an American company's latest technologies—software code, hardware designs, chemical formulas, you name it. If it has value, someone somewhere will try to steal it.

The United States is the only industrialized nation that doesn't allow its intelligence agencies to steal technology for the benefit of their domestic companies. So it isn't always nefarious nations stealing U.S. trade secrets; it is everybody, friend *and* foe.

In the 1970s, the CIA was surveilling two foreign bad guys who would only talk in an open field away from other people. If anyone approached, even an innocent bystander, the pair would quickly flee in different directions. Suspicious behavior to say the least. So the Agency needed a listening device, a "bug" in spy parlance, to hear what the conversation was about.

They engaged an entomologist, an insect scientist, to design a flying listening device that could approach the pair without arousing suspicion. After a brief flirtation with a bumble bee design, the entomologist returned with a plan for a dragonfly (Figure I.1).

This laser-guided, rocket-fueled drone was designed to mimic the speed and flying pattern of a real dragonfly. The prototype was soon followed by a production model that exceeded the required specifications. Unfortunately, any wind over 3 mph was enough to overwhelm the reaction time of the control system and the drones were never used operationally.

Figure I.1 **CIA dragonfly drones**

But this "successful failure" went on to influence the Agency's innovation protocols for decades.

It was a success in that it met the specified requirements but was a failure because it didn't solve the problem. The lesson point that developed was that the problem wasn't with the results. It was with the requirements that were originally created for the project. It was the failings of those who created the requirements that missed an assumption as simple as wind blowing across an open field.

Few government agencies like people documenting their failures— who would? Yet it's important to cite such projects because, as with many areas of life, we often learn more from the supposed failures than we do the successes. Managers don't engage the correct stakeholders, don't properly research it, and don't understand the problem they are trying to solve. They simply dictate *their* solution; market evaluation be damned!

They are usually quite good at detailing requirements, unfortunately those requirements don't accurately reflect the realities of the market-place. Many a corporate innovation project has drowned in a sea of finger-pointing from this. So does that mean we should put early product designs to our customers for them to decide? Maybe, but not so fast....

VivaTech is Europe's largest conference for start-ups and innovation technology. In 2021, they held their fifth conference as the Covid-19 pandemic was just starting to wane. Owing to the continued travel constraints from the virus, many of the speakers appeared by video link. Among them was Apple CEO Tim Cook.

Apple is one of the most successful corporations on the planet by any measure. Interviewed by film producer Guillaume Lacroix, Cook touched on several topics of interest to start-up entrepreneurs, including the importance of failure. He described his simple but insightful feelings on it, telling Lacroix:

> *Failing is a part of life. And it's a part whether you're a new startup or you're a company that's been around for a while. If you're not failing, you're not trying enough different things.*[1]

He went on to describe how Apple *allows themselves to fail*; that it is not only allowed, it is *expected*. Apple, he said, prefers to fail internally versus externally, because they don't want to involve customers in a product failure. Leadership greenlights many products for development beyond the laboratory, only to pull the plug later because the results don't meet the user experience, market size, or market demand the way Apple wants it to.

This is the head of one of the world's most technologically advanced companies. Tim Cook has not merely emerged from the shadow of legendary founder Steve Jobs, he has successfully led Apple down new paths that Jobs could barely have imagined. Cook appreciates that invention is about gazing into the darkness of uncertainty and racing ahead.

I'll put it another way: If you haven't failed at *something*, you'll never succeed at *anything*!

CHAPTER 1

A Recording Studio Is the Consummate Start-Up Incubator

A recording studio is where a creative product—music—is monetized. Studio time, renting both the equipment and the people to run it, starts at hundreds of dollars per hour. It's very similar to working with a good patent attorney, who likewise has a staff of expert paralegals and application specialists.

I've always thought that the walls of a start-up incubator should be lined with framed copies of the patents they've helped entrepreneurs secure, copying the gold and platinum albums that typically decorate a recording studio's walls.

Both are spaces with dedicated equipment staffed by teams of experts. Both maintain extensive networks of outside professionals in supporting roles such as accountants, managers, and designers. Both also provide advisors in finance, distribution, and licensing.

At the end of the day, a recording studio and an incubator are in the same business—they simply do it in different fields. Perhaps one of the most famous, and in many ways *infamous*, recording studios in the past few decades was Sound City outside Los Angeles, California.

Opened in 1969, the building had previously been a manufacturing plant and warehouse for the British instrument company Vox. Not long after becoming a studio however, Sound City's discolored walls were covered with framed platinum albums of the music recorded there.

This was the epicenter of music in the 1980s—if it played on pop radio, it was likely recorded there. Just a short list of alumni artists includes Tom Petty and the Heartbreakers, Metallica, Fleetwood Mac, Rick Springfield, Cheap Trick, Kansas, Guns-n-Roses, 9 Inch Nails,

Red Hot Chili Peppers, Nirvana, REO Speedwagon, Johnny Cash, Barry Manilow, Tony Bennett, Ratt, and Neil Young.[1] Some of the most iconic music of the period was recorded at this single, exceptional place (Figure 1.1).

Figure 1.1 A sampling of albums recorded at Sound City

But let's not kid ourselves, the place was a dump! Every artist, asked about Sound City, would say how nasty and dark the joint was. But they also noted it was not a place they went to for parties or hanging out—they went there to have the brightest minds in the business help them with their craft.

Many of today's more well-known music producers got their start at Sound City. You'll find them listed in the liner notes of those iconic albums. These people are brand names within the music industry. Names such as Nick Raskulinecz, Keith Olsen, Rick Rubin, Jimmy Iovine, and Butch Vig. (Ok, you might know Jimmy Iovine, but only because he and Dr. Dre sold Beats Music to Apple in 2014 for $3B, then helped launch Apple's streaming music service.)[2] But other than kudos on album sleeves, most producers remain blissfully anonymous.

Keith Olsen was an engineer turned producer at Sound City who passed away in early 2020. While an engineer's role in recording music is straightforward enough, a producer's role in the process is a bit more nebulous. Few have ever been able to describe the job adequately until Olsen put it simply as:

> *A producer's job is to get the artist's creativity into a form that is accessible to your market.*[3]

Olsen's words are poetic in their simplicity and eloquence. I came into working with start-ups from a career that began in the product development lab of a large corporation and later moved into market intelligence. We've always said that market intelligence was seeing through the customer's eyes—market strategy was knowing how to act on that understanding (Figure 1.2).

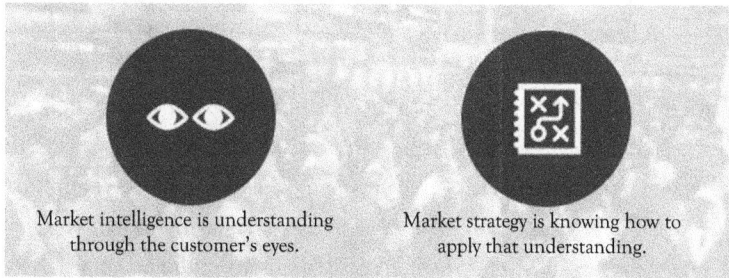

Market intelligence is understanding through the customer's eyes.

Market strategy is knowing how to apply that understanding.

Figure 1.2 Market intelligence and market strategy

A comprehensive study of failed start-ups reveals some startling statistics: Thirty-four percent of the failures were due to poor product–market fit.[4] Another 22 percent were the result of the ill-conceived marketing approach the start-up chose. That means over half of start-ups go under because they failed to follow Keith Olsen's advice about getting the creative product into the correct form for their market!

With a band, this is about gauging what an audience's interest would be for what the producer is hearing. Some producers may also be artists, but they are primarily people with great insight as to what specific segments of a market want, or would at least be willing to try, given the right product. That is their role.

What Olsen describes is precisely what the staff of a good incubator or accelerator does. They help entrepreneurs define what they are creating, be it a product or service. They force founders to articulate vague concepts in concrete ways—ideas can't simply be imagined into existence. They must be nurtured, developed, refined, and turned into something real. While cover art, distribution, and licensing agreements are not especially sexy, they are nonetheless how intellectual property (IP) is monetized. Getting entrepreneurs to that point is what incubators do.

Graduating from engineer to producer, Keith Olsen, (and others on a similar career track), slide to the left of the timeline, moving upstream in the creative process from tactical support at the mixing board's final stages, to strategically advising artists earlier in the process as the work itself is being envisioned. This is a much harder job.

As noted in the *Sound City* documentary by Dave Grohl (*Foo Fighters*, *Nirvana*), telling a successful artist like Tom Petty that their new song isn't quite up to snuff takes some thoughtful diplomacy. Nobody wants the hired help calling their baby ugly! It requires a level of tact, respect, and trust that can be quite challenging for all involved.

Many artists retain specific producers who've helped people they know or produced work they respect and want similar results. Other times it is the record label themselves, (the people paying the bills), that request a producer to provide adult supervision for inexperienced new talent. When you have the rare opportunity to compare an artist's original product to what was finalized after the producer's guiding hand, the differences can be stark. A rebuke from the producer might sting a bit, but results speak for themselves.

Rick Springfield describes how (producer) Keith Olsen selected a particular song from his demo tape.[5] Olsen felt the song had more potential than the others but was not enthralled with Springfield's guitar playing. He brought in a "hired gun," a studio musician named Neil Geraldo, who had just finished up recording with Pat Benatar at Sound City. Geraldo met Springfield, learned the song, and quickly laid down the track. *Jessie's Girl* hit #1 on Billboard's Hot 100 and earned Springfield the only Grammy Award of his career.[6]

This is what an expert pair of hands, (eyes, ears, ...), can do for a creative, be it an aspiring singer or an entrepreneur. They are more than a content confidant—these are people employed specifically for their ability to dispassionately evaluate a new concept in ways a creative may simply not have the time, energy, or experience to do on their own.

The Steve Jobs of Audio

In 1979, musician and producer Brian Eno delivered a keynote speech in New York. Entitled "*The Studio as a Compositional Tool*," he outlined how a studio can remix an arrangement in any number of ways not originally conceived by the composer.[7] He viewed the studio as a part of the creative process itself, not simply a place for recording it. The studio team was, for all intents and purposes, members of the band. And for him, the studio's mixing board was the instrument of their success.

Sound City's mixing board was one of a kind, hand built by an engineer named Rupert Neve. He was a creative visionary, volunteering for Britain's Royal Signals Corp (Army) in World War II at 17, owing to his gift in building and repairing radios.[8] After the war, he developed public address systems used by Princess (now Queen) Elizabeth and Winston Churchill. He was commissioned to build his first mixing board in 1960 and launched his start-up a year later.

Today, Rupert Neve Designs provides audio gear for some of the biggest names in music including Justin Timberlake, The Rolling Stones, Ariana Grande, Beyonce, Paul Simon, and Green Day.[9] The Guardian newspaper called him the "*Steve Jobs of audio*" after he passed away in February 2021 at the age of 94.[10]

"The Neve Board" as it came to be known, was an instrumental part of Sound City's success. Neve's overarching method centered around the concept of equalization, a process for balancing different frequencies within a sound itself, managing disruptive elements by raising or lowering individual pieces in real time. Engineers and producers could craft completely new variations for musicians to consider.

But like any instrument, the knobs and switches are powerless without talent at the controls. It requires a deft pair of hands, exquisite hearing, and a vision for the *art-of-the-possible*. Producers consult, cajole, and console musicians as many times as it takes to get the sound just right. The Neve Board might make the revisions possible, but it was a producer working with the artist who envisions what those changes can yield. As Brian Eno said, it makes them a part of the band and the creative process.

Modern digital recording gear means anyone can produce music by themselves in near studio quality at home. In some cases, even better quality. With Pro Tools and other digital software, instruments and voices can literally be perfect. So, why use a studio at all? Why pay someone to question your creation?

Mick Fleetwood said he first met Lindsey Buckingham and Stevie Nicks at Sound City.[11] Because of his relationships with the production team there, he formed the new Fleetwood Mac that we all now know. He pulled no punches on the realities of the creative process from both the artist and industry's perspectives. He talked about the desire by some artists to be left alone to create. Fleetwood said:

> *The downside is thinking "I can do this on my own." Yes, you can, but you'll be a much happier person doing it with others.*[12]

I remember thinking when I first heard this statement that it reminded me of something I'd read somewhere else and it took me months to figure out where. As it turns out, it was a book about start-ups. Reid Hoffman, the founder and CEO of LinkedIn, wrote:

> *No matter how brilliant your mind or strategy, if you're playing a solo game, you'll always lose out to a team.*[13]

That bit of insight speaks to the heart of what a professionally run incubator does. Creation is a team sport, as no individual can master all the various tasks necessary to get the job done right.

And while many might want to romanticize how music shouldn't be a business, it's simply not realistic. If an artist wants their work product where people can enjoy it for free, then simply perform in the park or give away self-recorded music CDs on street corners. But if they want to make a living with it, selling t-shirts and touring the world, then it is a business.

Business requires a thoughtful approach to ensure that all the disparate players involved, (musician and otherwise), are held to a professional standard, properly compensated, and their rights protected. This requires contracts, distribution agreements, royalty payments, tax and estate planning, and sharing the final product with others who helped it get to this stage.

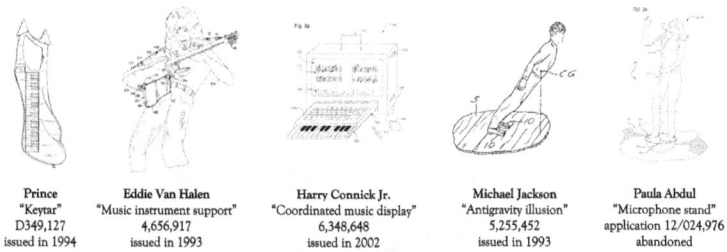

Prince	Eddie Van Halen	Harry Connick Jr.	Michael Jackson	Paula Abdul
"Keytar"	"Music instrument support"	"Coordinated music display"	"Antigravity illusion"	"Microphone stand"
D349,127	4,656,917	6,348,648	5,255,452	application 12/024,976
issued in 1994	issued in 1993	issued in 2002	issued in 1993	abandoned

Figure 1.3 Well-known musicians who are also lesser-known inventors, with images from their patent applications

Music artists understand this after a few years of struggling on their own, and the successful ones embrace it, concentrating on the creative process and leaving the business aspect to professionals. In doing so, their artistic energies can expand into new areas, creating other new revenue streams. This includes in technology.

Several successful musicians are innovators as well. Kanye West, Michael Jackson, Paula Abdul, Harry Connick Jr., Prince, and Eddie Van Halen aren't simply world-class musicians; they are also inventors with patents (Figure 1.3). And as with their music, it's not something they do by themselves.

Each had a dedicated team help them take a vague concept and turn it into another IP they can present to the market. So whether you want to play like Eddie, dance like Michael, or sing like Paula, the resulting product has to be in a format *acceptable to your market*; just as Keith Olsen said. Being good at one thing doesn't make you *automagically* good at doing something altogether different. The right team makes this much easier.

The lesson we can draw from Sound City specifically, and the music business in general, is that IP may be difficult to value and that value can certainly change over time, but it is an entrepreneur's best friend! Start-up founders building tomorrow's businesses must understand how to document, sell, and account for the IP they are creating.

Ziggy Stardust Sets the Stage

In 1997, David Bowie partnered with Prudential Insurance to raise $55M in corporate bonds by offering investors the income from his collection of 25 released albums.[14] Within the portfolio was some of Bowie's most famous work, including *Heroes*, *The Man Who Sold the World*, and the iconic *Ziggy Stardust*.

The bonds had a face value of $1,000 at an 8 percent interest rate maturing in 10 years. It was one of the earliest uses of IP as investment collateral. It was also ideal for investors seeking a low-risk, steady-return vehicle not subject to wide yield fluctuations.

Two decades later, more firms are offering similar "musical notes" to underwrite investment products, including the performance rights organization SESAC, which owns the music rights on albums by Adele, Neil Diamond, and more.[15] Other IP is being offered in this way as well, from the wellness chain Massage Envy to the automotive firm Driven Brands.[16]

I don't know if it was Covid-19 keeping everyone at home listening to music that sent the industry into overdrive, or if all the artists, (and a few of their producers), suddenly saw the light of Bowie's brilliance. But from early 2020 to the present day, music-based IP portfolios have become very hot. Bob Dylan, Shakira, and numerous other artists are licensing their rights portfolios for big payoffs, many to multinational corporations able to further monetize those properties.

Music's IP value has an underlying importance every start-up CEO should understand—he or she *is replaceable*. Thirty plus years after they began Journey replaced Steve Perry with Arnel Pineda. Queen replaced the late Freddy Mercury with Marc Martel and then Adam Lambert. Van Halen replaced David Lee Roth with Sammy Hagar. Foreigner, YES, and Motley Crue have embarked on very successful global tours with new lead singers at center stage.

The music plays on because that IP typically belongs to an entity, not an individual. Start-ups are very much the same. Like a lead singer, a founding CEO may only be right for that initial creative stage. If Steve Jobs can be fired from Apple,[17] a new start-up CEO can be removed as well, but "the band" will play on. With start-ups, it is not uncommon for someone else to step in with the skills to scale globally. Other times, companies acquire the IP and take it far beyond what the original artists conceived, extending it past the creative's lifetime.

Last year music publisher Primary Wave acquired an 80 percent interest in Stevie Nick's songwriting catalog, a property they valued at around

$100M.[18] The same firm acquired a controlling interest this year in the estate of Prince, (his likeness, image, and music), valuing the overall IP portfolio at between $100M and $300M.[19]

Monetizing IP is the future of business. If you're not doing it now, start-ups could easily be your ticket to long-term revenue streams like these music catalogs.

CHAPTER 2

Intellectual Property Is the Primary Corporate Asset

I know what you're thinking. That's all fine for musicians, but why should Corporate America care? Why all the banter on intellectual property (IP)? Well, as it turns out, big corporations have the exact same interests as all these musicians.

Back in the 1980s, corporate assets were things like real estate, manufacturing facilities, and big machines for building stuff—heavy equipment that was expensive to buy, labor intensive to maintain, and generally impossible to move once it was set in place.

This is what created the company towns of the industrial age—once a manufacturer had a site up and running, everything else just sort of popped up around it. Not simply suppliers and partners, but entire cities as people moved to where the jobs were. Now, however, everything has changed.

Companies no longer have long-term physical assets on their accounting books. If you look at S&P 500 companies, their assets are largely intangibles (Figure 2.1).

What's behind this radical shift? It's several factors, from technology to markets to demographics to economics. But these influences are forcing change on how corporations operate. As we all know, big companies don't generally change willingly, so this transformation has been slow and hard fought. But that's not really a surprise.

Tangible assets are physical things. They can be visited, (real estate and buildings), touched (machines and equipment), and stored (products and merchandise). Because they're so visible and apparent, they are relatively easy to quantify. What is this piece of land or that large machine worth? Depreciation tables for valuing assets over time are simple, commoditized

Components *of* S&P market 500 value

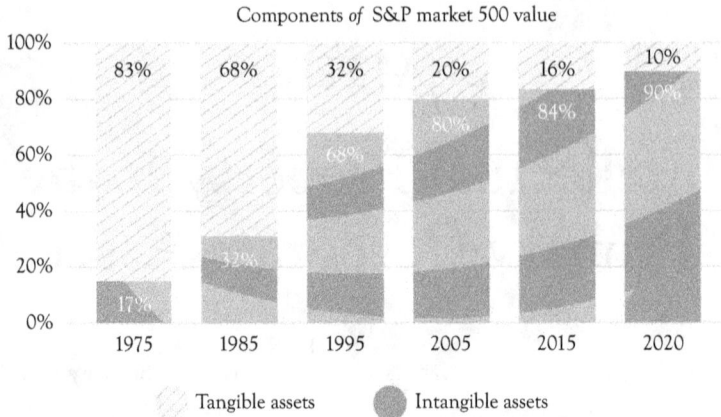

Figure 2.1 Company assets of tangible versus intangible property according to Ocean Tomo, a part of J. S. Held

Source: Ocean Tomo, a part of J. S. Held, intangible asset market value study, 2020.

to a point where any second-year finance student can account for them reliably. Unfortunately, those easy days are now largely in the past.

So what are these *intangibles*? What does that word even mean? It means IP and can encompass a wide array of matters: Business methods, exclusive platforms, new technologies, proprietary algorithms, custom software, brand image, patents and pending applications, registered trademarks, copyrighted literary works, industrial trade secrets, product distribution networks, and supply chain contracts, just to name a few. Valuing, or more correctly *monetizing* those assets, is an entirely different skill set from managing physical assets.

The commercial world has become more virtual in ways most of us never anticipated. We mocked things like Second Life and other consumer video "games" that refashioned the real world through Internet-based virtual scenes, never realizing that our largest corporations were racing toward that same model right under our noses. These one-off assets, previously derided by Finance Departments as their "island of misfit toys," are now the foundations of corporate value.

One unexpected aspect of this change is mobility. I can move a company easier than I can move my own home. As many of the contracts are also digital, (instead of archived physical paper), they too can be sent anywhere in the world in milliseconds.

A home and family however are another matter. A residence is a tangible entity. Children still require tearful goodbyes with friends. Movers must come pack belongings into boxes and load them onto trucks. While all of that is occurring, I can move my company from here to there with a laptop, possibly even from a smartphone!

This is having a pronounced impact on companies large and small. In business school, they teach the Four Ps of Marketing. These are Product, Price, Placement, and Promotion. For a physical-asset world these made sense:

- **Product**: Describe what the product is or does, (detergent, automobile, or shirt), and why the consumer will want it.
- **Price**: How much will the item cost, (purchase, maintenance, and upgrades), and how it compares to competitive products.
- **Placement**: How will customer buy the product, (retail, wholesale, or discount), will it be in individual packets or only in bulk.
- **Promotion**: How will customer learn of the product, (TV, radio, or print ads), and where should those ad placements be segmented.

This was how business was conducted for decades, and like the finance/accounting model cited previously, everyone was comfortable with it, understood it, and largely knew their place in it. That has all changed.

Work *product* isn't the only thing that is mobile. Work *location* has become mobile too. Witness the 2019/2020 Covid-19 pandemic. Many people lost their jobs, while many more, if not most of the American public, turned to working remotely from home.

Our children were learning remotely too, often underfoot or in an immediately adjacent (and loud) room. While parents were meeting with colleagues via Microsoft Teams, the kids were adjusting to remote classrooms via Zoom video. For those without fast, wide bandwidth Wi-Fi at home, this was a frustrating time.

For some, the problems still exist as returns to work and school have been uneven across the country. State and city governments have taken wildly different strategies in restarting economies at the local level. For many, resources were already stretched thin. The pandemic's emerging Omicron variant has exacerbated this.

It created not just inequalities in results, but it has also highlighted fundamental new disincentives for employees looking to make a change. If I can start a company anywhere, why shouldn't I start it in the most favorable location possible? As a start-up entrepreneur, my intangible assets—patents or contracts or copyrights—can all fit on a USB drive. The question becomes, *where do I want to live?*

This is unfamiliar territory for local governments. For years, economic development offices dangled tax incentives and labor rebates to entice corporations to place a new facility in their municipality. That meant jobs and spillover economic benefits, which improve the private economy and the government tax base.

Disparities in regional economic growth are well documented.[1] But state and local tax incentives designed to spur development have largely failed in recent years.[2] Three billion dollars (each) in subsidies were offered to Foxconn in Wisconsin[3] and Amazon in New York,[4] only to become high-profile PR disasters. Kansas and Missouri agreed to quit outbidding each other after $355M in incentives only netted around 1,200 jobs in state-swapped relocations.[5]

Now, economic development offices have four marketing Ps of their own to entice IP-centered companies. These are Professional, Proximal, Personal, and Psychological. But in an increasingly work-from-home (WFH) world, these are focused on the needs of the people, because that is how cities now measure success. To wit:

- **Professional**: As an entrepreneur, my professional needs are low start-up costs, complementary industry clusters (such as medical, manufacturing, or metadata—meaning fast Internet), and a deep talent pool coming out of local universities.
- **Proximal**: What does a city offer in pro or college sports, live music venues and auditoriums, or cultural arts via theater and museums that we can enjoy in our off hours?
- **Personal**: How safe and secure is the city? Are there riots or random shootings? If so, we'll move on. What is the cost of

housing and basic utilities? How good are the education and health care options in the area?

- **Psychological**: How are my political and spiritual needs met? Do nonprofit organizations think globally and act locally here? Is innovation a mindset or is it simply painted on the walls?

Some states and municipalities have real trouble in these areas. There's been an ongoing migration away from long-time employment strongholds, a situation that was further enflamed by the Covid pandemic. California had a net loss of residents for the first time in decades. New York has seen quite a few people, and even entire corporations, leaving the Big Apple citing high crime, taxes, and housing costs.

In 2019, Alliance Bernstein CEO Seth Bernstein told the crowd at Nashville's 36/86 Startup Conference that he was moving the company from New York City to Music City because he'd realized his own daughter couldn't afford to live in Manhattan.

She'd just graduated from college and despite all the advantages he could provide, she couldn't afford to live on her own locally. He realized that most of his employees were in far less advantageous positions. How would his firm be competitive for badly needed IT and cybersecurity talent if no one can afford to live there? Something had to change, so he decided to lead it. He moved the company and took as many employees as he could with him.

An extreme measure? No doubt, but it's indicative of the change that is taking place. Alliance Bernstein is a finance company in description, but a technology company in practice. Without talented IT staff it has no business at all.

Seth Bernstein recognized this and wanted first-mover advantage relocating to a livable city that had a solid base of future employees graduating from college. He was not alone in his analysis. Amazon became a close follower, taking their ill-fated New York headquarters plan and instead locating it in Nashville.[6]

So what do both firms have in common? Their primary assets are IP! Alliance Bernstein's financial holdings can be managed from anywhere. Amazon's e-commerce infrastructure is similarly operated virtually, with the spillover effect of repurposing dozens of former shopping malls into fulfillment centers close to their customer base.[7]

Cities are taking notice and making changes to accommodate this need. Chattanooga, Tennessee has been working on their start-up ecosystem for years, building upon a city-owned fiber optic network with the fastest Internet speed in the country.[8] Once derided as the dirtiest city in America,[9] it is a great example of hybrid thinking: Small town community for employees and big city infrastructure for technology start-ups. TimeOut.com, Travel & Leisure, and PC Mag are but a few of the international press outlets that have praised the city as a top WFH and start-up destination.

Chattanooga is not alone with its quality-of-life approach. Up the coast in Pittsburgh, Carnegie Mellon University (CMU) President Farnam Jahanian has also recognized the importance of start-ups to the local economy. Jahanian acknowledges that despite working to be on par with other entrepreneur-focused universities such as Stanford, MIT, and Harvard, the community has struggled to keep CMU start-ups in town.[10] He's trying to change that.

Pittsburgh could be Chattanooga's older brother. Both are river-based cities with long manufacturing legacies being transformed by education and medical technologies. Both cities have mountains, a kitschy incline railway, and downtown innovation districts. Both take their bridge architecture seriously and have beautiful hiking trails full of waterfalls. Both also have a singularly unique start-up draw—CMU in Pittsburgh and supersized Internet access in Chattanooga.

Cities such as Chattanooga and Pittsburgh are rolling out the red carpet for entrepreneurial talent. The shift to corporate IP assets means that while companies are competing for employees, cities are competing for where that talent will live! They want to concentrate those assets for the exact same reason companies do—to enjoy economies of scale. Quality of life will be the competitive differentiator for cities for the foreseeable future.

If lots of people, (what companies call "*their most important asset*"), are congregating into quality-of-life cities, big corporations will have to move quickly to monetize these employee-assets before a competitor does! There's no longer a geographic limit to the depth of talent and technology a corporation can reach in working with entrepreneurs. Cities are reacting to this by flipping the incentives around. Some municipalities are offering to pay remote workers up to $20,000 to move to their city.[11] Why? Because the long-term value of that citizen's salary has a significant impact on the local economy.

This means start-up investments may not be just out of your industry, they can also be out of your zip code. IP investing brings new opportunities for corporate leaders with the guts to take a leap. Three great examples would be:

- **Mezi**: Conversational artificial intelligence for call center operations would be attractive to many retail companies. American Express struck fast, acquiring Mezi in 2018.[12]
- **Mirror**: A gymnasium that takes up the floorspace of a ruler! Lululemon invested after realizing people working out at home still need something to wear.[13]
- **Ntwrk**: Youth culture and video-based e-commerce elicited Footlocker to make an investment after seeing opportunities for original content and exclusive products.[14]

Entrepreneurship Inside

The same is true for existing employees a corporation has now. People already on the payroll are forcing a re-examination of Human Resources policies in the face of a top talent exodus. Depending on how employment contracts are written, the corporation may not own the IP rights to technology not directly relevant to their current business interests. Rather than allow employees to leave and start their firms why not partner with them?

This creates spinoff opportunities, internal start-ups that gain enough traction to leave the corporate umbrella and take on a life of their own. Contract manufacturer Flextronics did this a few years ago with two software assets; a supply chain service called Elementum and a construction industry joint venture called YTWO. In 2018, a UBS research note predicted the two IP-based start-ups could be worth $2B in a couple of years.[15]

The entertainment business has benefited from this strategy for years. Music, movies, and live sports are all intellectual properties monetized through licensing, copyrights, and franchises. Spinoffs and merchandising properties are their lifeblood, from *The Fast and the Furious*, to Marvel and DC Comics, to whatever film number *Star Trek* has now reached.

Own the IP and you can generate income for decades!

CHAPTER 3

What'll It Be? Incubator, Accelerator, or Venture?

So now that you've decided you want to do "something" by working with start-up companies, what then shall you do? That largely depends on your comfort level in risk, cost, and accountability. Are you prepared to fail? Are you prepared to fail and not hang an executive out to dry as a result? If not, finding volunteers is going to be considerably more challenging.

Before deciding who is going to run this project, you must first decide exactly what it is going to entail. Do you want to incubate start-ups internally, from within your own ranks? Do you want to partner with an accelerator—either with local government, nonprofit foundations, or universities—and keep the start-ups at arm's length? Do you want to provide more than help—do you want to participate, or perhaps even lead funding with some innovative companies?

Muddling through these questions may cause a lot of hand-wringing, but it needn't be a problem. Company executives, (and their Boards), can easily decide on what they are most comfortable with and simply pick a starting point. Keep in mind—this is NOT carved in stone. If the company/Board/employees don't like one direction, you can pivot to one of the other options. You are committing to try, nothing more, so take it in that spirit.

There are five dimensions to work through in deciding how you want to approach tackling this question. They are dimensions in that each is a distinct but interrelated layer in the questions you are going to ask the stakeholders within your firm. These are Structure, Function, Process, Information, and Time. Let's define each so we're all on the same page.

1. *Structure*—identify the components (mainly the people) involved in the effort. This includes everyone involved, inside the company and

out, detailing what their roles are, (and *aren't*. You don't need any Monday morning quarterbacks in this.) What are the relationships between all these players in the effort? Do they know each other already, do they get along, can they work effectively together in a potentially stressful environment?

2. *Function*—define the desired outcomes of the effort, what result is the company looking for? What decision making is going to be required; who makes those decisions and based on what input? Are these individual decisions or is it a group effort? What approvals are necessary and how will those be managed and documented?

3. *Process*—what is the sequence of steps for managing the effort? What are the layers of approval in decision making? (How is Legal involved for instance?) How is the approval process documented for the company, who is the spokesperson, and what information is shared versus held in confidence?

4. *Information*—what data is created from this innovation effort? Who does it belong to? What is the process for securing patents or trademarks? Who manages these efforts? How are they paid for and maintained? Are there Joint Research Agreements in place contractually with internal or outside start-ups?

5. *Time*—where is the company's attention focused, in the past or toward the future? (Both have their place, but it's helpful if everyone is looking in the same direction. This will largely depend on the strategy being pursued.)

Every company will have disagreements on these dimensions, and that's to be expected. Whomever is in charge will need to corral the various stakeholders and get the fencepole sitters into the game even if they disagree on the direction selected. You will not get unanimous agreement, so take that fantasy off the table right now. Figure out what these dimensions entail and then select one of the following three models. Do you want to *Cram* a lot of knowledge into founders quickly, *Create* new innovations with experienced business people, or *Compete* head-to-head out in the marketplace?

Incubator Model

The incubator model is the most common, but in some ways also the most difficult due to the time commitment required (Figure 3.1). With this you are typically working with young start-ups—by young I mean started by young people, 20-somethings without a lot of life experience, to say nothing of a lot of business experience. Their learning curve will be built through on-the-job training as they iterate their vague idea into a business. So for each dimension listed previously, there are specific ramifications to them and to those supporting them.

This requires a great deal of *structure* between the start-up founder and the corporation. Put less delicately, they need more handholding. If they are an employee already (an intrapreneur) this can speed things up a bit. If they are an external founder, you're speed dating to say the least! Because they are likely inexperienced in business, they may not know the differences between working capital and operating capital. Corporate support will be needed from finance, accounting, human resources, legal, and more.

The corporation's *function* in the relationship will be to provide as much information as possible to the start-up's core team. This includes all the support mentioned previously, and yes, the start-up's founders will be drinking from a fire hose. They'll likely want some market research assistance, as well as some corporate communications help in using that market research. In addition to starting their business, they are also absorbing all the stuff you are trying to teach them. Free hours will be few and time management will be paramount to make this work.

The *process* of questioning your young protégés means your questions will be directive in nature. Theirs will be too. Both of you are trying to steer the course to a certain degree, but that doesn't necessarily mean you are fighting over the helm. You, (as the corporate innovator), want to keep them out of trouble and they, (as the young Turks), want to damn the torpedoes and go full steam ahead. They should be able to question you without questioning your authority, and you should be able to query their assumptions without being condescending. A little patience here goes a long way!

The *information* flow is primarily in one direction, (toward the start-up), as they've the most to learn comparatively speaking. Taxes, city/county permitting, financial planning, and a host of other issues they don't even know exist, await them. Oh, and they've still got to get their prototype designed and built! Despite the huge stone they're rolling up the mountain, it's a hill that every young start-up has had to climb, and they can reach the summit too.

Time may seem to pass very slowly (for them) as they are learning, but they get the benefit of your experience. All those areas to address (taxes, permits, etc.) that might frighten a young entrepreneur are old hat to many inside a big corporation. Permitting instructions from the county Environmental Protection Agency (EPA) office may appear to be written in Greek translated from Klingon as far as a new entrepreneur is concerned. But it's the native tongue for an experienced corporate Safety, Health, and Ecology manager. Allow these pros to use their experience and spend a few hours helping a start-up launch quickly, economically, and safely.

The incubator model is popular with universities, as they are already focused on education and many have dedicated research offices staffed with lawyers to handle patent applications and licensing contracts for start-up IP. One of the more famous examples of this is Gatorade, which has generated >$250M in licensing, (about $12M annually now), for the University of Florida.[1] This is a success story many organizations would love to copy.

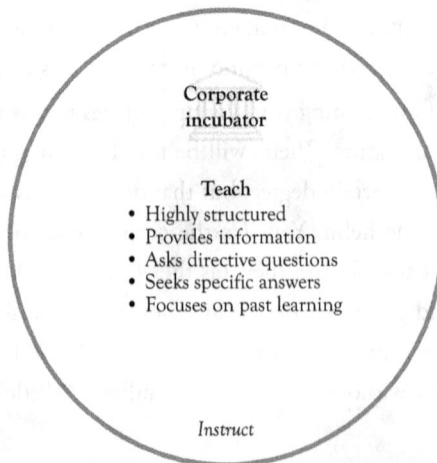

Figure 3.1 Incubator model

Accelerator Model

The second model available to a corporation for working with start-ups is that of a mentor. Here you are not forging the knife from raw iron, but are instead sharpening the blade. I like to say you are helping them hone their craft. This is a popular arrangement a corporation will embrace when a start-up is in an adjacent field, perhaps not a competitor (yet) but one that can benefit from the corporation's expertise and knowledge.

This means the *structure* of the relationship may not be as tightly wound as with the incubator model. The start-up founders likely have either (1) some industry experience, so they don't have quite the learning curve of the prior example, or (2) they have an innovation that is so radically different that it upends the current "normal" for the industry and needs further development before it can succeed.

This honing of craft means many current *functions* may no longer be necessary if the start-up is successful. Perhaps steps in a manufacturing process will be eliminated. This could significantly change the cost structure to a product and make it cheaper, or perhaps change a batch process to a continuous process. Maybe this reduces production time, dropping it from days to hours, perhaps even a single shift.

This change to the normal *process* will elicit praise and condemnation equally. Those who prefer *"the way we've always done it"* will heap derision upon the start-up's plan. This is a defense mechanism more than anything else, as those folks feel threatened by the start-up's potential impact. Embracing change can be difficult, but is necessary if things are to improve.

Start-up founders are pushing this change and in doing so will seek new answers to their questions. They want this new *information* to help them formulate better questions in the future, derive additional insights into their customers, or at least determine what future products or services those customers might want from this new offering. How, when, and where that information is stored, collected, and analyzed may draw interest from the corporation, as it's a potential advantage they've never had before.

The start-up will be delighted to leverage the corporation's *past* experience so they don't repeat some of the same mistakes. That doesn't mean they won't make new ones of their own—they most certainly will. But by not repeating your past snafus, they can grow faster, better, and financially leaner than they could on their own.

Accelerators are popular for companies seeking improvements to important processes ahead of competitors (Figure 3.2). Walmart, for example, operates three accelerators in different functional areas and plans to open two more. For retail innovations there is Store # 8 in Hoboken, New Jersey. An e-commerce accelerator in Austin, Texas, leverages that city's considerable tech talent. In 2019, a new accelerator focused on payment processing systems named TailFin Labs was created in partnership with Green Dot. In March 2022, the company announced new technology hubs in Atlanta and Toronto, hoping to leverage both city's talented work forces, particularly in artificial intelligence.[2]

Figure 3.2 Accelerator model

Venture Model

When a company starts directly funding new start-ups, they're jumping into the deep end of the pool. This is a real commitment as it's using real company dollars to fund new innovations created either internally or externally. Corporate Venture Capital can be enormously successful, but like the other two models, it's important to know exactly what risks and opportunities the corporation wants to take.

"Hold on loosely," a song by the band 38 Special, is a great way to characterize the *structure* for corporate funding of a start-up. The song continues *"if you cling too tightly, you're going to lose control."* True enough. It's called arm's length for a reason—connected to the body yes, but not close to the chest. Manage it accordingly. If you invited suppliers or customers to invest as well, you could be accused of taking too much of a guiding hand in the operations if something goes wrong. Try to avoid that.

In financing a start-up's seed round, you want to give them plenty of rope to make their own mistakes without allowing them to hang themselves in the process. Your *function* here is like that of a parent overseeing a child. You've provided an allowance and you want to make sure the money is not frittered away on something stupid. So, if your new start-up promptly purchases naming rights for the local college stadium with your funding you are justified in interceding.

The *process* by which you take such actions is, again, slightly different than the other examples. You have considerable control over the start-up as the financier, probably a Board seat or similar management controls. Depending on how the deal was constructed, you might be able to remove the founder or CEO unilaterally. That's a very different relationship than through an incubator or accelerator. Corporate governance is in play here, where again, based on the deal structure, you might have a controlling interest in how the start-up is exited; either an acquisition, an Initial Public Offering (IPO), or a Special Purpose Acquisition Company (SPAC). The point is, you're far more involved in overall strategy.

How is *information* from the start-up used in such a close relationship? If you have the same customers, are you sharing information between you? Do the customers know that? Many states are following California's example and creating data privacy laws. Some countries are doing the same. If data is physically stored on a server in state or country "A" can you legally access it from state or country "B"? China's new Data Security Law is very different from Europe's General Data Protection Regulation (GDPR), so consulting a data privacy lawyer with international experience is a wise investment.

Customers might simply assume you and your start-up are sharing data, so you cannot overcommunicate enough when this is NOT the case. You want start-up and customer relations to be similar in their long-term nature, but nonetheless separate. This was an investment in your over-the-horizon strategy, your future, so don't allow misinterpretation to screw things up for any of you. This is like baking a cake, and as any chef will tell you, it cannot be rushed. Transparency is your friend here.

With Corporate Venture Capital you are coaching. Think about it—do Bill Belichick or Nick Saban teach or advise their athletes? Do they ask politely, with sugar on top? No, they direct. Coaches are paid to do one thing—win! They apply psychological tools to help determine the coachability of the players they are considering. If a player is not coachable, they are likely not investing in them. Start-ups aren't much different.

This is about competition—knowing who it is, preparing for them, and then executing when the game is on the line. Corporate Venture is for those who eat, drink, and breathe rivalries (Figure 3.3).

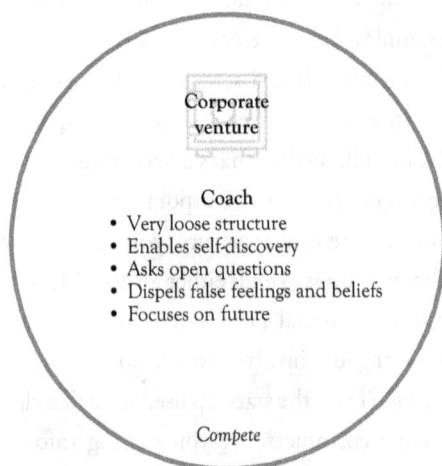

Corporate venture

Coach
- Very loose structure
- Enables self-discovery
- Asks open questions
- Dispels false feelings and beliefs
- Focuses on future

Compete

Figure 3.3 Venture model

What you must remember is the competition isn't just for the start-up, it's for the corporation as well. You are now elevating the game against your industry peers. You aren't just coaching a little start-up; you are also pitching your corporate brand against other big firms who similarly want to be in the venture space. It's not just the start-up's street battle—it's also yours. When they get cut, you bleed!

Those Aren't Olympic Rings!

At the beginning of the chapter, I suggested the three models are related and that is true. Each is distinct in its own way, but they all share several attributes, and not just the five dimensions that I outlined.

Incubator and accelerator efforts are similar in how they are tailored around specific skills and processes. This is something a new start-up entrepreneur may (or may not) already know, but as their teacher or mentor it is your responsibility to ensure they get it.

Accelerator and venture efforts are similar in how your corporate assistance is tailored around functional needs. The entrepreneur is no neophyte—they understand business and likely a good bit about their industry. They need to ramp up their ability to compete effectively in the marketplace.

Finally, ventures and incubators share a unique similarity in that their services are tailored to individual founder's needs. These are widely opposite ends of the spectrum to be sure, but whether it is coaching a prize fighter or teaching a kid how to lace up the gloves on day one, everything is personalized for that individual at that time and in that location.

What all three share is a desire to build something new (Figure 3.4). A new product, service, or business where before there was nothing. Entrepreneurs need help in each of these areas as they develop a business, and if everyone remembers the role they are playing the chances of success are much, much better.

Milquetoast corporate cowards will argue that periods like our present financial turbulence are not the time to launch a start-up. History would disagree. In San Francisco, amidst the chaos of the 2008 Wall Street crash, a company named Airbnb was founded. Uber launched in early 2009, followed immediately by WhatsApp and Pinterest, with Instagram close on their heels in 2010. Overseas, Delivery Hero (Germany), Careem (Dubai), Byju's (India), Paytm (India), Didi (China), Gojek (Indonesia), and Trax (Singapore) are just a few of the prominent start-ups founded during the same period. It's a matter of leadership and will.

Coca-Cola had a successful incubator, but when profits slipped it was cut off as a cost savings measure.[3] Casio briefly had an incubator,

Corporate
venture

Corporate
incubator

Coach
- Very loose structure
- Enables self-discovery
- Asks open questions
- Dispels false feelings and beliefs
- Focuses on future

Tailored to
individual needs

Teach
- Highly structured
- Provides information
- Asks directive questions
- Seeks specific answers
- Focuses on past learning

Desire
to
build

Tailored to
functional needs

Tailored to
skills and processes

Mentor
- Structured
- Provides information sources
- Answers direct questions
- Seeks alternate answers
- Focuses on past experiences

Corporate
accelerator

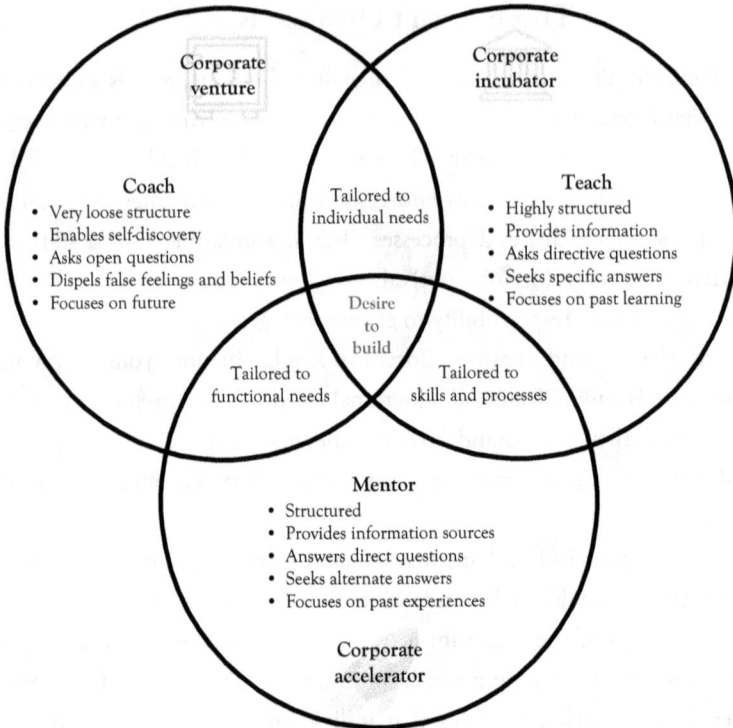

Figure 3.4 Three overlapping models

but had no champion linking the Silicon Valley team to leadership based in Japan.[4] Whether an incubator, accelerator, or venture office, it has to have support from the very top. Otherwise, it (and any other innovation effort), is doomed to failure.

Xerox PARC invented the laser printer, but executives sat on it, not wanting to poach their own product line. They paid dearly for that short-sightedness. Perhaps more famously, Kodak invented the digital camera after 15 years of R&D but refused to commercialize it, compelling their own bankruptcy in 2012.[5] It was such a colossal management failure that Harvard Business School has published several case studies on it.[6]

Whom you choose to run this effort will determine its success. Are you passing this off to just anyone or are you bringing in your own Nick Raskulinecz, Keith Olsen, or Butch Vig as your producer? The bottom line is people matter more than money, technology, or markets. Deciding who will run your program is far more important than deciding which start-ups will participate.

CHAPTER 4

Getting Your (Start-Up) Foot in the (Corporate) Door

So let's say you're an innovation manager looking for a start-up to acquire or partner with. Better still, you're a start-up founder wanting to attract the attention of a potential corporate suitor. How do you begin such a conversation? What brings the two entities to the table?

It's not as hard as it appears. Formally, big corporations don't like talking about the work they are doing. Informally, they are oozing information all over the place. So for start-up founders it is simply a matter of doing some homework, a bit of digging here and there, and assembling the puzzle pieces enough until you can see an emerging picture.

Sometimes that picture tells you straightaway that a particular corporation is not going to be interested in whatever you are doing. Alternatively, you might find that a company you'd otherwise dismiss entirely is searching for precisely the solution you are proposing, but you would never have imagined reaching out to them. So how do you start?

First, understand what the corporation is really interested in—put aside for a moment what their website might say or even what their Public Relations people are putting out. Instead, dig into their financial documents. Look deep into a public company's annual report and see if it spells out where they are spending money. Is there an R&D line item in the financials? Great! Drill into that a bit online.

Another good source is Wall Street. Publicly traded companies, and now quite a few private ones, are covered by analysts writing research products on these companies. This includes everyone from the big banks like JP Morgan and Goldman Sachs, to specialty houses that invest privately, to industry products on health care or technology published by firms like Raymond James & Associates. The analysts at these shops are typically approachable, their e-mail addresses and phone numbers readily available, and are happy to chat about the companies and industries they cover.

As for the corporations themselves, check out their employees on LinkedIn. People, especially R&D or product development types, love to talk about what they are doing. The specifics of their work should certainly be confidential, but you'll see some broad strokes in their profiles. If they are an electrical engineer, are they specialists in broadband fiber optics? Wi-Fi communications? Electric vehicle (EV) battery systems? Then obviously the company has some interests in these areas.

Look also at conferences and conventions. Anybody speaking or presenting a paper—*especially* those presenting a paper—is worthy of checking out. In many instances, they proposed a stage-based keynote address, but instead were downgraded to only presenting a paper. That paper is likely to reflect what they are working on at their employer. Again, consider the technologies being researched, the products being designed, and the markets targeted to find where a corporate or start-up partner can be found.

Check out local and regional press for general business and industry-specific publications. Their reporters often have a good ear to the ground as to what companies are doing—perhaps not in stated investment targets, but certainly in the types of technologies (or help) they are looking for. Most are happy to give you a lead in the hope of getting a scoop if the partnership succeeds.

There was recently an unusual example of young start-ups being pushed out of the nest to find new corporate investors. General Electric (GE), a stalwart of American business, has fallen on difficult times leadership-wise. Owing to a series of poor management decisions, the company decided to liquidate one of the best corporate venture capital shops in history. Launched in 2013, GE Ventures was pieced apart to try and pare down a $110M debt the parent company was facing.[1]

No corporate division wants multiple start-ups on their Profit and Loss statement. GE Power, for instance, doesn't want to interfere with its turbine business, but it needs a renewable energy strategy. By investing in start-ups at the corporate level, GE Power gets access to new IP and business models; keeping them close, but not interfering in the larger (profit-generating) business. The same was true in health care, transportation, enterprise computing, and mobility. GE's strategy was successful because it was a corporate-based portfolio and manufacturing focused; a win–win at both the enterprise and division level.

For years GE Ventures was the gold standard of corporate venture investing, particularly in the manufacturing arena, where it was frequently copied but never equaled. Now however, the party was over, and GE wanted to sell off the portfolio en masse.

But that did not happen. Few manufacturers have the exact same interests or as wide a variety of industry verticals as GE. The portfolio covered medical devices, aviation equipment, computer servers, energy systems, a variety of data services, and much more.

In the end, the portfolio was sold off in pieces. Among the buyers were Leerink Revelation Partners, which purchased 16 of the health care start-ups,[2] and 40 North Ventures, which bought 11 of the industrial companies.[3] But with over a hundred firms in the portfolio, it was a long process.

GE Ventures provides a great mix of different types of start-ups we can play with in a theoretical exercise of how others might attract corporate investors or buyers. One thing that buying a portfolio from another entity provides is access to the other investors who participated previously in funding those start-ups.

If you are new to the incubator or Corporate Venture world, this is a great introduction to future investing partners who might come in handy later. Let's look at just four of the companies in the GE Ventures portfolio to keep the discussion manageable: Menlo Microsystems, Xometry, Foghorn, and Optomec.

- **Menlo Microsystems** provides improved size, weight, cost, and performance in electronic switch technologies, creating high-performance components for products ranging from battery chargers to medical devices.
- **Xometry** puts Big Data to work so customers can easily choose the optimal price/lead time option for their project,

providing access to the production capacity of over 5,000 manufacturers.

- **Foghorn** processes and analyzes diagnostic equipment and patient monitoring tools at the source, (edge computing), so medical facilities can optimize supply chain operations and enhance patient services and privacy.
- **Optomec** enables additive manufacturing technology to coexist with conventional manufacturing methods, embracing an open system approach to 3D printing that does not bind customers to a single materials supplier.

These are impressive young companies operating across multiple industries by providing a well-articulated value to their customers. Few companies invest in a vacuum and one as accomplished as GE Ventures is certainly no exception.

For some of the portfolio start-ups, GE was the original seed investor. In others, they came in later. For a select few, GE led the investing round, inviting other venture capital (VC) firms, partners, suppliers, and customers to join them. For current investors looking to acquire start-ups from this portfolio, these firms provide a fine means for kick-starting a new corporate relationship by taking several steps at once (Figure 4.1).

Figure 4.1 Other early investors in four of GE Ventures start-up portfolio companies

No matter which of these young firms a company might be interested in, they're going to find themselves with some pretty impressive investing partners. Corning, BMW, Honeywell, and Bosch. The Defense Department. There's a lot to be said for buying assets from an entity like GE Ventures, as all the initial, (*ahem*: difficult, time consuming, and expensive), due diligence has largely been done.

Among the benefits to a company acquiring a fixed portfolio like GE's is the ***di***vestment opportunities. GE might want to bundle some in groups based on industry, technology, or market to speed up the liquidation process. But it is equally likely any of those groups might include a start-up or two that is not a long-term interest for an acquiring firm. Fortunately, those other prior investment partners may have right-of-first-refusal options for divestment.

As the buyer, you can likely sell the original investment to these, (or another partner of your own), even with an additional markup for your time and effort. The current investors have the most to gain or lose, and their terms were probably not as good as GE's. So in addition to the start-up partnerships you are gaining, you can now (1) create positive relations with these other investors and (2) reallocate the funds from those one or two sales into other start-ups you are interested in.

This is not different from what professional sports teams do in "selling" athlete contracts to each other—trading is a common, everyday occurrence. We create the bench depth for the team we want, not the team we inherit from someone else. It's nothing personal; if it is not a good fit, you're doing both parties a favor in splitting up.

So, looking at our four start-ups here, let's consider what areas in common a theoretical corporate entity might have with them. What if that corporation was, like GE, a manufacturing firm? Let's assume your corporation was spending R&D money on a few select technology areas; perhaps adhesives, analytics, camera optics, and 3D printing. We'd come up with a chart like the one shown in the following figure (Figure 4.2).

One of the start-ups, Foghorn, has technologies in two areas your corporation is investing in—data analytics and optics. So if you are interested in acquiring a couple of start-ups, Foghorn is going to quickly rise to the top of your list. Why? Because your company is already investing

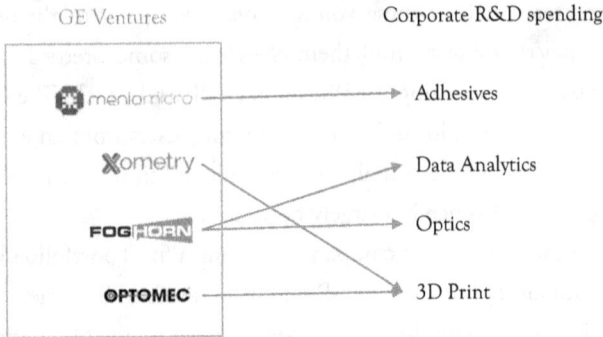

Figure 4.2 Investment areas

in these two areas. If Foghorn has technologies you can leverage, they gain (1) a new customer as well as (2) a potential new partial owner to invest in them further.

Look at Foghorn's other investors—Bosch, Honeywell, Dell, and so on. There may be opportunities to work with those companies in a collaborative manner. Assuming they are not a direct competitor of yours, these are firms with outstanding research departments that a potential start-up investor now has a legitimate reason to engage with. Foghorn is looking better and better, because it expands the reach of your R&D to adjacent corporate partners with whom you previously had no relationship.

Existing Customers

Past the R&D question, the next area of interest a big corporation might have in a start-up is what customers do they share? The customers, either by contractual requirement, discretion over planned product developments, or simply by being in another division or product line, might not have ever mentioned (or for that matter, even know) that they are customers of both your big corporation and this small start-up.

Look at our four GE Ventures start-ups. Despite being in radically different businesses, they have a lot of cross customers just among themselves! These are some global brand names. If the start-ups are servicing these clients, they must be doing something right.

So if your corporation has three divisions—automotive, aerospace, and electronics for instance—you would have reason to be interested in all of these start-up firms. That doesn't automatically mean your company should acquire them, but you should certainly give a lot of thought to what might happen if your biggest competitors were to acquire one of them instead!

Would that put your business in jeopardy? That will certainly be worth discussing at the highest levels. So it's no longer a question of *"do we want to acquire this startup?"* Now it must also be asked if *"we should ensure competitor XYZ cannot acquire this startup?"* What is the present value of the start-up's revenue with your customer worth versus the future value of losing that customer if the start-up is acquired by a rival? Let the Finance Department play around with those scenario models for a while.

Every corporation wants to get more revenue from the customers they already have; that is, they want to increase their *"share of wallet"* from them. This is what built Amazon. From selling just books they now sell many things, capturing more share of wallet by offering items customers were previously buying from other retailers (Target, Walmart, …).

Big companies will readily talk to a start-up with whom they share a big customer, making that conversation a lot easier! Properly positioned, such a conversation can make both the start-up and the established corporation look better in the customer's eyes. The corporation might be seen as being more innovative, more customer focused, and looking more toward the future with their relationship.

The start-up is seen as validating its business model by such an investment or acquisition by the corporation. It now has access to more resources without adding to its overhead with new hiring, purchasing real estate, or expanding its physical footprint. The potential corporate parent likely already has that, giving the start-up access to its resources at virtually no cost, keeping the start-up's prices low. The corporation can now also bring in its extended network of suppliers, partners, Board of Directors relationships, and other customers, expanding the start-up's potential revenues at an accelerated pace (Figure 4.3).

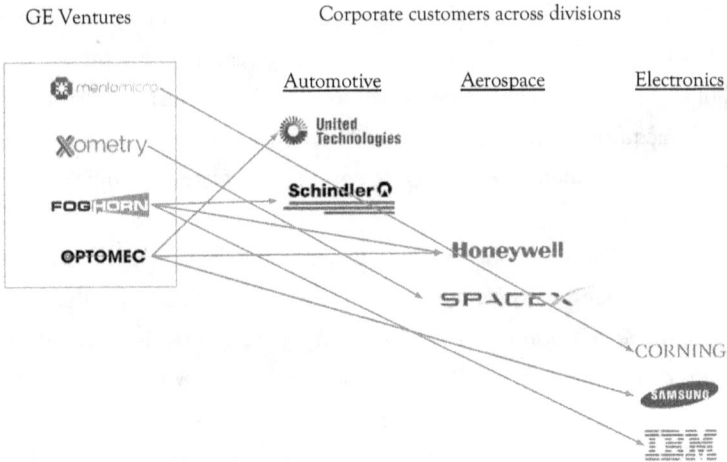

Figure 4.3 Start-ups and common customers

Aspirational Customers

It's a simple fact. Some doors just refuse to open. Beg, buy, borrow, or steal, sometimes you just can't get a purchasing manager to meet with you. It's frustrating. It's not like you called the guy's mother a bad name. He simply refuses to give you 30 minutes to hear why your product is better than, stronger than, or faster than the supplier he has now. You've tried it all and he simply won't budge.

Then, this little nobody of a start-up shows up at your door. In a gracious gesture you allow the poorly dressed, barely out of college knuckleheads to come into your marble and oak-framed boardroom to pitch their firm. One meaningless slide after another, a seemingly endless stream of palpable nonsense pours from the screen. For this you went to Harvard B-school? To be pitched by a trio of t-shirt wearing ....

Wait a minute!

What the hell was that? You jump up in the chair and ask them to back up to the previous slide. Never mind if the poor guy has to restart his monologue again, you must be sure.

Click!

Yep. There it is. The Nobel Prize, the Lombardi Trophy, and Olympic Gold all rolled into one. The Logo Above All Logos.

This miserable little start-up serves the very same purchasing manager who refuses to let you anywhere near him. They have unfettered contact with this guy, and likely also his R&D department, logistics staff, shipping and receiving, and so much more. They have the one thing all your corporate benefits cannot provide: *Access!*

The trio of cofounders starts talking again, once more advancing to the next slide, but you have mentally checked out. Oh, these lucky bastards! They could be Moe, Larry, and Curly for all your care, but you're going to find a way to ensure your company partners, purchases, or participates in future funding with these guys. Because the Stooges, for all their lack of polish today, can give you what you've dreamed of tomorrow. Year-end bonus here you come! In your head you are already sipping *mai tais* on the volcanic black sand beaches of Maui as your kids snap pictures of Christmas palm trees. *Happy New Year* indeed!

For our quartet of GE Ventures portfolio start-ups, one name in particular stands out for a theoretical corporate manager. Xometry has five customers your corporation has coveted for years, and with a simple investment action you could have direct access into these firms (Figure 4.4).

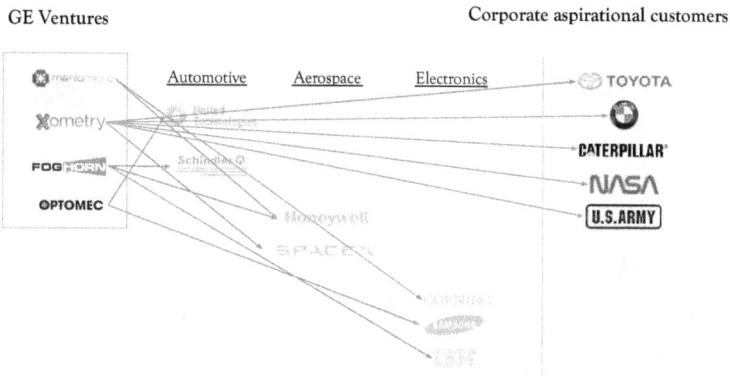

Figure 4.4 Start-ups and aspirational corporate customers

These companies are likely in different business divisions, so this will not be a simple pop-and-drop effort. But any quick call to one of the division presidents will likely garner an encouraging e-mail to the Chief Financial Officer (CFO), General Counsel, or whomever else might need a gentle prodding that this start-up is worth pursuing.

This shows how even the smallest of start-ups can entice a potential corporate parent to invest, acquire, or partner with them by offering what the parent company has, thus far, been unable to gain on their own. Looking at what start-ups you, (or perhaps your competition), have as high-potential target customers is an excellent means for selling the idea of a company incubator, accelerator, or Venture Capital effort.

CHAPTER 5

Corporate Venture Capital

In January 2020, the successful TechStars accelerator in Detroit announced it was shutting down.[1] The original sponsor firms—Ford, Honda, Amazon, Lear Corporation, Nationwide, and Microsoft—chose to end their funding for the project. The fact each firm has a separate Corporate Venture Capital (CVC) office gives us a pretty good indication of why.

Ford's internal incubator program has locations not just in nearby Dearborn, they also have about 30 people split between London, Toronto, Los Angeles, and Palo Alto. Honda Innovations has an "Xcelerator" program operating in the United States, Canada, and Japan.[2] Amazon, in addition to its long-running Lab 126 R&D facility,[3] recently launched a $2B venture fund for transportation and energy projects.[4] Microsoft's M12 Venture Fund,[5] Nationwide Ventures,[6] and Lear Innovation Ventures[7] round out the group. You get the idea.

So here's the problem. Ironically, when Detroit TechStars began in 2015 it was called TechStars *Mobility*, intending to draw attention and business to Detroit. It was successful in that effort. What changed was the automobile industry. Yes, Ford and Honda are technically competitors in the consumer vehicle space, though the TechStars programs wouldn't have incorporated any of their present business.

But the automobile business is no longer about building cars. It is increasingly about the mobility business, (like I said, *ironic*). Or as CNN put it, automakers are now in the technology business.[8] That transformation put all six sponsors into competition for employees, platform designs, business models, and certainly for who will store, control, and analyze data in this new mobility space.

Seen in this light, it makes sense for the sextet to part as friends rather than have any conflicts of interest or contested intellectual property (IP) suddenly explode onto the front page of *The Wall Street Journal*.

Mobility refers to everything in, on, and around a vehicle; passenger or commercial, consumer owned or ride-share hired, moving people or cargo. The data volume is crazy, and in this respect, all six firms would be in the untenable position of sharing within TechStars everything they were competing for outside of it in the marketplace. Breaking up may be hard to do, but sometimes it is the right thing to do.

So here are six very different companies, with different histories and cultural norms, all of whom are operating CVC offices. Before I describe some best practices these groups may follow, let's get a few disastrous practices out of the way first, just so those don't get any traction inside your firm.

How do we separate start-up interests from traditional Corporate Development work? Aren't those guys the ones in the M&A business? Yes, they are. But we're not talking about Mergers & Acquisitions. We're talking about long-term risk taking.

Corporate Development acquires companies that are, well, *a sure thing*. Known entities; competitors, suppliers, customers, or firms in adjacent industry or technology fields. These firms are called "going concerns." They have a history of revenue and profits, proprietary technologies or patents, market access in some region or industry that is attractive, or they add a significant value to a corporate acquirer's current structure, (*aka* a vertical integration strategy).

Corporate development officers know how to bring in Wall Street financiers, folks from Goldman Sachs and Deutsche Bank. Their rolodex includes a multitude of outside legal counsel that specializes in integrating one company into another, assimilating their real estate, labor contracts, and current customer deals to make "*them*" a part of "*us*."

Corporate development's results are expected to be seen in immediately subsequent operating quarters or they will face Wall Street's wrath. With start-ups, we're looking way into a future that nobody can quite make out yet. We're all looking at the same horizon, but from a different perspective, requiring a very different mindset.

They are digging around for *facts* about those firms. But with start-ups, you are looking for *truth*—the truth about a new technology, a new business model, or a new way of approaching an old problem. Market intelligence professionals like to say they "*trade in the currency of ambiguity.*" That is the whole reason the function exists, to reduce uncertainty in competition. It is also why large corporations leverage their market intelligence teams to evaluate start-ups.

Start-ups are built on a foundation of uncertainty. The kinds of risk that send corporate development professionals screaming into the night is precisely what gets entrepreneurs out of bed every morning.

So, can global corporations and local start-ups coexist? Yes, absolutely, they just have to remember they are not the same. They are not equal and that is the whole point. Big companies have teams of professional staffers, while start-ups have trouble just attracting talent. A big company spells out the rules in black and white, while in start-ups everything is in shades of grey.

Everyone participates in multiple ways, from pitching customers in the morning to pitching out the trash when they finally go home at 10:00 p.m. *Shark Tank's* Lori Grenier once said, "*Entrepreneurs are the only people who will work 80 hours a week to avoid working 40 hours a week.*"[9] She's right. These people want to do something more and they are looking for opportunities. If your company won't help them find it, be assured your competition will.

Three Key Points

CVC does not operate the same way as traditional VC firms. A typical venture investor often seeks to "pump and dump" a start-up—put money in quickly and get it out just as fast, generally seeking a 10X multiple on the investment. By contrast, CVC's primary interest isn't financial, it's strategic.

CVC officers want insights on future trends, the development of future industries, or establishing the "*canary in a coal mine*" warning system for their leadership. The focus is not on immediate cash returns, but instead on what is changing in the market. For this reason, return horizons on CVC capital are typically 7 to 10 years out; over twice as long as ideal VC timelines.

There are three critical points to consider when deciding on whether to launch a CVC effort. First is to understand the opportunity that exists here. Some in a corporation's leadership will mistakenly believe any effort to do something like this puts them in direct competition with marquee firms like Kleiner Perkins or Sequoia Capital. That's an understandable, but largely misguided concern, particularly these days.

Research by Cambridge Associates has shown that seed investing is where 74 percent of venture capital returns have historically originated.[10] Yet in 2019, Pitchbook estimates only about 7 percent of VC firms are presently engaged in (prepandemic) seed rounds,[11] choosing to focus on later-stage opportunities where the funding amounts are larger even at the lower returns.

In a 2022 research note, Pitchbook analyst Kyle Stanford cited how micro-funds (<$50M each typically) have raced into this void. He notes many of these new funds have set up shop outside the traditional venture capital strongholds of New York, San Francisco, and Boston. There are over two hundred micro-fund venture capital companies in the United States, and more being created every day.[12]

These new firms are specialty start-ups seeding other start-ups, disrupting the traditional venture capital model completely. This new competition has marquee firms scrambling to create new funds just for seed purposes to ensure their future pipelines, with Andreessen Horowitz raising $400M and Greylock Partners setting aside $500M (Figure 5.1).[13]

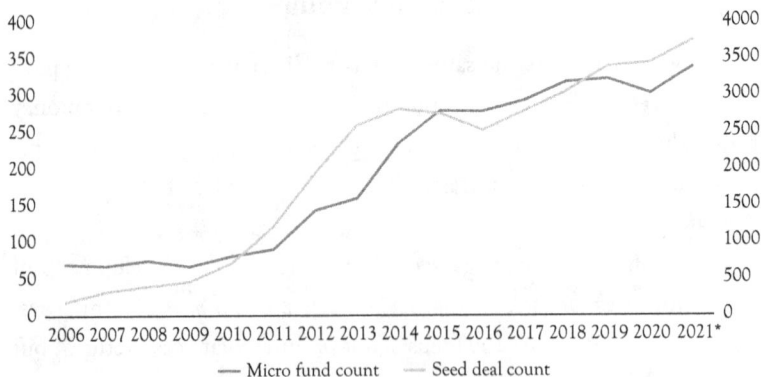

Figure 5.1 Seed deal count and micro-fund growth

Source: Courtesy of Kyle Stanford and Pitchbook.

Micro-funds seed early-stage start-ups with investments that are generally smaller than traditional capital firms, focusing on between $25K and $500K.[14] Lest you think a start-up can't succeed from such humble amounts, Uber received micro venture funding from Lowercase Capital[15] and DropBox got early investment from SV Angel.[16] Capital is no longer an impediment to launching a start-up—whether it is inside or outside a corporation.

Traditional venture capital firms don't fear competition, they fear missing out on opportunities. They aren't concerned about losing money, but they are concerned they will be making less than the next VC firm; it's a kind of financial *Blood Sport.* As a result, they have too many competing opportunities to wait around on seed investments to pay off. They want results now. So there are real opportunities for corporate shops to engage in early-stage seed investing—keeping that longer term perspective in mind—inviting Kleiner or Sequoia to join in later.

Why would they do that? Because traditional VC firms prefer to put a lot of money in later stages than a little money in early ones! It seems crazy, but they'll forgo early opportunities to have time, capital, and mental bandwidth to jump in later for a (perceived) less risky payoff.

Again, this points to that significant difference between traditional and corporate venture capital. Corporations pursue strategy, traditional investors pursue payoff. Fortunately, this does not put them at odds. Quite the contrary, it can make them very favorable business partners when they find the right opportunities.

The second major point is that seed rounds now have more opportunity for markup than ever before. Because the traditional venture capital organizations are not participating in seed funding as they once did, the market for corporations, family investment offices, and other nontraditional seed investors has never been better, (hence the growth of those micro-funds).

For start-ups, this provides a variety of new financing and equity-sharing opportunities that likely will not be as arduous to negotiate as many of the traditional VC firms can be. (Put another way, an entrepreneur is not as likely to have to give up majority equity and control with these investors as they might with Silicon Valley VC brands.)

For seed stage investors, choices abound for the type and nature of investments that are in demand. VCs cannot offer follow-up Series A and B investments if start-ups can't get launched in the first place. Corporate investors will likely invest seed money in nearby start-ups where they can keep an eye on their money. This is good, as venture firms increasingly look beyond the San Francisco Bay area where housing, taxes, and labor costs are exceptionally high for would-be start-ups.[17] Eighty percent of seed financing deals now originate *outside* of Silicon Valley.[18]

Finally, the third significant point is CVC has grown to where it is a legitimate player in funding young, innovative companies. What was once only the purview of international firms such as Apple and Google is now available to any company with the guts (faith) and grit (leadership) to take it on.

Former America Online CEO Steve Case toured the nation advocating Middle America entrepreneurship, writing a piece for *The Wall Street Journal* on how innovators were moving off the coasts into the nation's rust-belt interior. Case hopes this meant fewer "*photo-sharing apps*" and instead, more solutions to real-world problems.[19]

Historically, big tech companies kept their corporate venture capital efforts focused on the West Coast. But as more of these firms have expanded across the country, they are finding numerous local innovators with ideas and technologies that should be pursued. These idea "collision points" are where many new start-up companies originate.

The Wall Street Journal noted cloud data center demands are creating new technology centers nationwide.[20] Northern Virginia has emerged as the East Coast center of gravity for cloud computing, with regional operations also popping up in Texas, New York, and Connecticut.

Google is spending $10B on new cloud operations in nine states from Arizona to Georgia. Adobe and Apple are building facilities in North Carolina and Texas, while Facebook and PayPal have set up shop in Utah. As big tech players expand eastward, their CVC team's influence expands with them. In 2018, for the first time, corporate venture shops participated in over 50 percent of all venture funding.[21]

The legacy technology firms do not have an advantage over any other corporate venture group, other than the fact they've been doing it longer and have more experience. For corporations looking to get into the game, talking about it is not the same as doing it. Yes, there will be failures, as Tim Cook so aptly pointed out earlier. But one thing that is for sure is these technology giants understand they must be willing to make mistakes.

Jeff Bezos has just stepped down as CEO from Amazon as this book was being written.[22] Like Cook, Bezos understands that failure is part of innovation and long-term strategy. In his 2019 letter to shareholders he wrote, *"If the size of your failures isn't growing, you're not going to be inventing at a size that can actually move the needle."*[23] If that's not good enough, a trio of other billionaires—Sara Blakely, Elon Musk, and Richard Branson—have all said the same thing—success requires getting past that fear of failure.[24]

Seed-stage start-up funding needs have been voiced by entrepreneurs from Oregon[25] to Virginia.[26] But funding is not the only need start-ups have. Even small and midsized companies can proactively participate in their local start-up ecosystem by offering office/lab space, customer introductions, and even short-term specialty labor, (engineers, software developers, etc.).

Such forward-leaning firms attract thought leader employees, see higher internal returns on R&D, and improve employee retention. Start-ups spinning out from one corporate entity are more likely to attract attention from another entity looking to expand, acquire, or advance into adjacent technologies.

And let's not limit this to U.S.-based start-ups. Just because a corporation is U.S.-based doesn't mean it can't link up with start-ups overseas. There are many foreign incubator, university, and local accelerators that would welcome American corporate partners. They are as interested in our market as U.S. companies are interested in theirs. If ever there was a win–win situation, this could be it, particularly for smaller American companies looking to expand.

Many companies seek to have additional U.S. offices, while some want international operations. Recall the prior chapter's overview of General Electric's venture portfolio; several of those firms had multiple offices. Let's take a quick look at three of them.

- **Tamr** is a data cleaning and formatting firm for human-guided machine learning. It has offices on both coasts—Seattle and San Francisco to the west, with Boston and New York on the east.
- **Theta Ray** is a cybersecurity and data analytics firm based in Israel, but also had offices in New York and Singapore.

- **Maana** is a knowledge management platform for organizing industrial data and human expertise to help make faster decisions. Their U.S. offices were in Seattle, Silicon Valley, and Houston. But they also had offices in London and in Saudi Arabia.

As with any start-up a corporation might want to invest in, the value of these firms is in their customer contracts, IP, and expertise, (their employees). What's unique about them is that despite their comparatively small size and short lifespans, they've got multiple locations in areas many U.S. corporations have no presence in. Investing in multioffice or overseas-headquartered start-ups is a way to expand presence, brand, and influence.

Corporate spinoffs may also be an option for small to medium-sized firms seeking to "spin-in" start-ups with new products, IP, and business models. Some firms will see start-ups as a differentiation opportunity, others will use such acquisitions to move ahead of an aggressive competitor. For others, the twilight of their product may be close at hand, and innovative start-ups can provide a head start into a bold new future.

CHAPTER 6

Strategy on a Page

Start-ups have traditionally used pitch decks to attract investor attention, often as part of so-called Elevator Pitch sessions. If you were riding up an elevator with investment guru Warren Buffett, could you pitch your start-up idea before you both reached the top floor? The problem with pitch decks is they are financial-focused. Because that is what traditional venture capital investors are interested in.

But as I've said, corporate venture capital is focused on strategy, not finance. The pitch deck that works for traditional VCs will mean less to corporate teams. Instead, start-up founders need to take a page from the corporate playbook and speak in the language they prefer.

Strategy on a Page, or SOAP, is a visual means for detailing a company, (or department, or group, or division), strategy to an audience in a clear and unambiguous way. This is a great tool for start-ups to use when pitching investors, partners, or employees.

Now to be honest, I hate PowerPoint. It is a storytelling crutch. Anyone can mask the lack of something meaningful to say by putting up a nauseating litany of slides to distract the audience as they ramble on. But the corporate world knows PowerPoint, understands PowerPoint, and embraces PowerPoint. There is no escape from it. So instead of replacing it, we'll turn this potential weakness into a strength.

Rather than a whole deck of slides, we'll use one. *One*. A lone canvas upon which you will paint the story of your start-up, (or of the start-up you want to acquire). Paradoxically, the beauty of this strategy is the freedom it provides. You can tell a story a dozen different ways depending on (1) who is delivering it and (2) whom the audience is.

This one slide works equally well for the CEO, the CFO, or the CTO. There's no need for multiple versions that invariably get mixed up. It works for speaking to investors, reporters, or to Aunt Jo when you're stuck sitting next to her over an extended Thanksgiving weekend. It is hard to screw up because of its simplicity.

I came up with the idea of applying SOAP to start-ups after watching a documentary on the venture capital industry, which included a section on Intel Corporation. My very first published article was on Intel's brilliantly innovative strategy for the Pentium chip.[1] I've harbored a nearly three-decade-long affection for the company ever since.

Two engineers, Gordon Moore and Robert Noyce, wanted to break away from Fairchild Semiconductor back in the 1960s.[2] Fairchild is the company that put the Silicon into Silicon Valley. Gordon and Moore wanted to move on and needed money to launch a start-up. So they went to a man named Arthur Rock, the guy who'd originally helped fund Fairchild.

When Moore and Noyce approached him they had no name for the company and no business plan. Arthur Rock was a New York banker, not a West Coast entrepreneur, so while he wasn't a founding father of Intel Corporation, he was certainly a contributing cousin. Rock told the pair he needed "something" he could give to potential investors. So Moore and Noyce typed out three double-spaced paragraphs on a single sheet of paper.

Here it is in all its glory. Arthur Rock wasn't a fan of lengthy business plans that founders wouldn't follow and investors wouldn't read. He wanted something simple and direct. It is easy to keep everyone on the same sheet of music when there is only a single sheet for the entire tune!

It was full of spelling errors, typos, and grammatical problems. Yet, despite this literary catastrophe, Arthur Rock raised five million dollars to launch Intel. But not every start-up entrepreneur has a financial genius and strategic visionary like Arthur Rock laying around. I assume that most, like me when I launched my first start-up, don't know any investment bankers. So what if we could instead craft a visual counterpart to Intel's three-paragraph epistle (Figure 6.1)?

We need to put five distinct types of information onto this one slide and it still has to be readable when we're done. This is a visual medium remember, so there must be leftover space for icons, logos, and things like

The company will engage in research, development, adn manufacture and sales of integrated electronic structures to fulfill the needs of electronic systems manufacturers. This will include thin films, thick films, semiconductor devices, and other solid state componenes used ih hybrid and monolithic integrated structures.

A variety of processes will be established, both at a laboratory and production level. These include crystal growth, slicing, lapping, polishing, solid state diffusion, photolithographic masking and etching, vacuum evaporation, film deposition, assembly, packaging, and testing, as well as the development and manufacture of special processing and testing equipmentrequired to carry out these processes.

Products may include dioded transistors, field effect devices, photo sensitive devices, photo emitting devices, integrated circuits, and subsystems commonly referred to by the phrase "large scale integration." Principal customers for these products are expected to be the manufacturers of advanced electronic systems for communications, radar, control and data processing. It is anticipated that many of these customers will be located outside California.

Figure 6.1 Intel Corporation's original three-paragraph business plan

that. Let's write out answers to the five questions first, then decide how to visualize the information afterward. We'll start off easy with something an impatient investor might ask. *Why are we here?*

1. What is this start-up all about? Sum it up in a single sentence—not even a complete sentence. Short and sweet, what is it about? Why are you taking up our time today? Why should we care?
2. What are the *founder's* priorities? What keeps them up at night, plotting? What problem are they trying to solve, and what are the three or four focus areas they will be looking at morning, noon, and night for the next several years?
3. What is the value proposition to customers? Why will they care? What is the customer going to see that makes them slap their foreheads and exclaim "*Why didn't I think of that myself?*"

4. How will the start-up deliver that value? (This was Arthur Rock's favorite area—how are you executing on the value cited earlier?) These activities MUST directly support the value proposition outlined in #3. Otherwise, rewrite them!

5. Finally, what brand image should form in the customer's minds when they think about the start-up? Is what pops to into their heads in sync with the founder's priorities outlined in #2 mentioned previously? If not, rewrite them until it is!

Again, the execution strategies (#4) must support the value you're selling (#3); and if you're effective, the mental image your brand creates *externally* (#5) will be reflected in the founder's *internal* priorities (#2). So, let's figure this out for Intel using nothing but the materials in Moore and Noyce's three paragraphs.

I like to put a picture in the background as a stage setter. This is purely theatrical however, so it's really up to you. For Intel I used a basic circuit board. But if you're meeting with potential investors or partners, it is nice to have a relevant image up on the screen before you even get started. Think of it as an entrepreneurial mood setter.

So what was Intel's basic premise? Look at the opening sentence of the business plan. "*Engage in R&D, manufacturing, and sales of integrated electronic structures.*" Structures. Not just semiconductors, which were Moore and Noyce's bread and butter at Fairchild. They wanted to expand and provide all the components consumer electronics brands would need for circuit boards.

Their target customers were Electronic Manufacturing Service companies. That makes sense—it's an industry they are already familiar with and that knows them. Liquids and circuits; what's that about? Well it turns out making circuit boards includes lots of thin films of liquid copper and other metals. There's also a lot of adhesives. While it's simple enough to have a human operator put a dab of glue on a transistor when you're making dozens of items, it's quite different to have a machine churning them out by the tens of thousands. That is rather difficult, but Moore and Noyce, fresh out of Fairchild Semiconductor, know a lot about that stuff.

They can speak eloquently about different types of technology and, as we know from Moore's Law, (yes, he's THAT Gordon Moore), the number of transistors doubles every two years, even though the cost is halved. The level of automation needed to keep up with that kind of rapid innovation is expensive and labor intensive. That's what Moore and Noyce sought to do—put economies of scale to work across a lot of different components and bring prices down so that customers would rather contract it out instead of making the required large capital investments on their own (Figure 6.2).

That parlayed into integrated technologies, going from semiconductors to resistors to capacitors and every other little gizmo on a circuit board. As these boards become more sophisticated they are more expensive to make, so the attraction of using an outside entity to manufacture them makes sense.

Customers could also outsource laboratory work to Intel, taking development ideas and commercializing them by keeping the labs running with legions of bench chemists and electrical engineers on the payroll. Once the development work was done, Intel could manufacture a new item as close to the customer as needed, even providing product testing to the customer's satisfaction, before packaging it up and sending it to *their* customer.

So what is the brand statement? Integrated circuits, smaller components, and expanding beyond computers into consumer electronics. These are easily digestible concepts that resonate with people in the target industry areas, addressing a known problem they all have.

Do the strategies support the GOAL plans for customers? Yes, it appears they do. Does the brand image in a customer's mind sync with Moore and Noyce's PRIORITIES? Yes, they do. Something like this is (hopefully) a little cleaner than Intel's three paragraphs.

For modern purposes, this same slide can be used by *intra*preneurs trying to show how their spinoff idea is distinct from the parent corporation's business model (Figure 6.3). For outside start-ups looking to get investment from a corporate partner, it can also demonstrate the many similarities the two companies might share. Strategy on a page can be Zoomed, e-mailed, or easily turned into a brief video clip that can be shared with other stakeholders as needed.

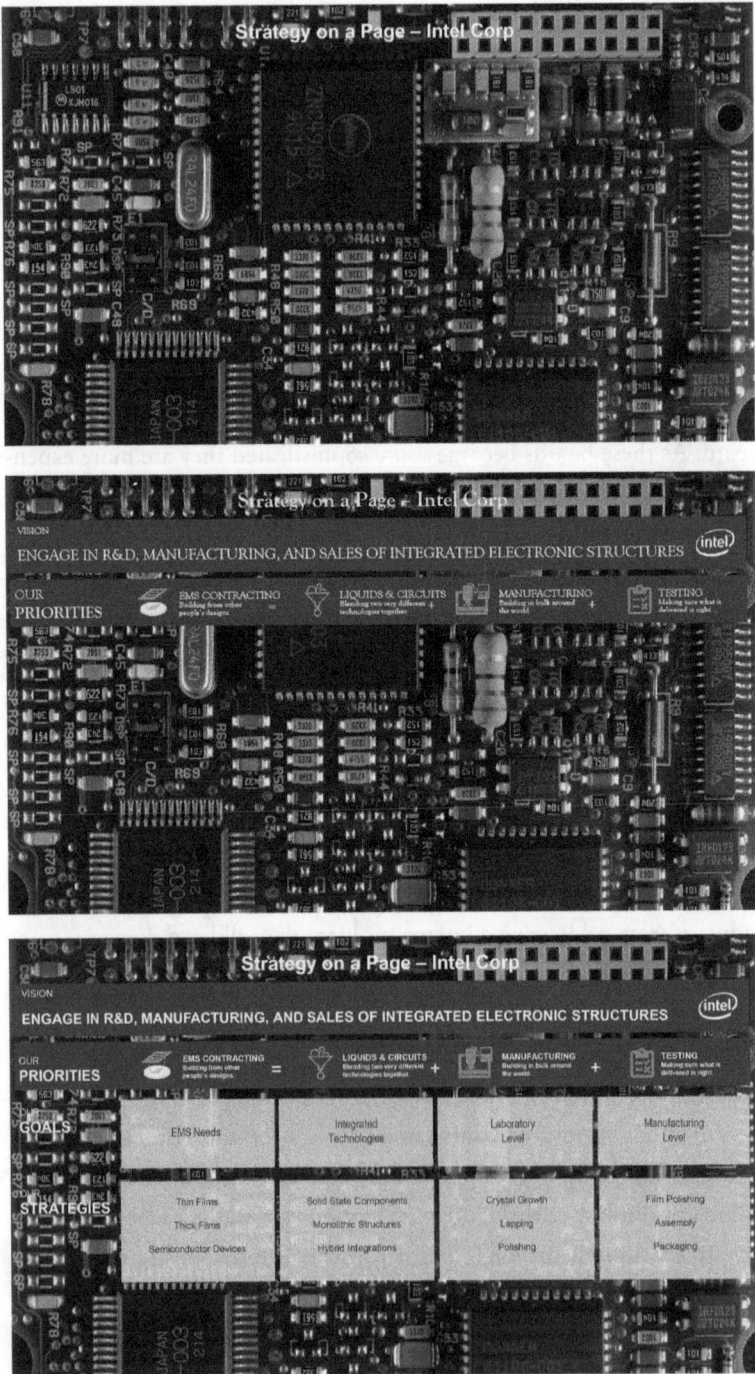

Figure 6.2 *Building a Strategy on a Page (SOAP) for Intel as a start-up*

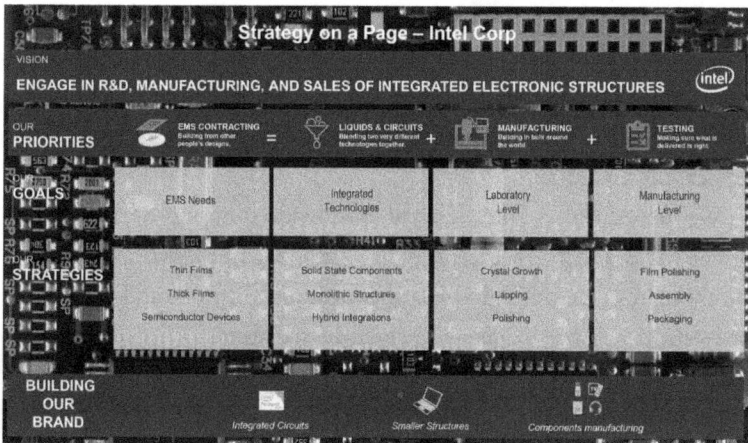

Figure 6.3 Finished Intel Corp (start-up) SOAP

Let me demonstrate it on something a little more personal. I launched my first start-up, Autography LLC, a bit over ten years ago. We created autographed digital memorabilia for authors, artists, and athletes. Our plan was to be the preferred management platform for maintaining a worldwide fan base. Rather than wholesalers and retailers taking all the profits, performers of every stripe would take fans with them as they switched publishers, recording labels, or professional teams.

We provided analytics for business managers to not only find new fans easily, they could reward them for spending money on game tickets, backstage passes, and other merchandise. The longer fans remained with the performer over the course of a career, the better their rewards would be. What did we offer? Personalized digital memorabilia, largely based on word of mouth, in a subscription model that only paid us when the artist made money.

Patents were our intellectual property (IP) of choice. How do you know Tiki Barber actually signed that photo rather than his twin brother Rhonde? Because our patented system mathematically measured the stroke of the stylus—the speed, curvature, or change of direction, and flagged it if it doesn't match—we had something very different from physical memorabilia providers. We could authenticate media on demand and archive it forever.

We patented other tech too, from Fantasy Sports to biometrics to streaming audio/video of the event. I went on a USO tour, autographing one of my e-books for troops across the Middle East, soon learning that other authors want to do the same. Publishers loved having e-book author events, and two professional sports leagues accepted our authentication tech as equal to the hologram sticker technology they were using for physical merchandise.

We helped the luddites, crafted worldwide licensing deals, and had former MLB and NBA executives on our Board of Advisors. So when you thought of us, our fail-safe authentication was front and center. For the celebrities, it was the analytics, and the social-media friendly product could be bragged about online across the planet. So, how do we digest all of that into a single slide? How about this (Figure 6.4).

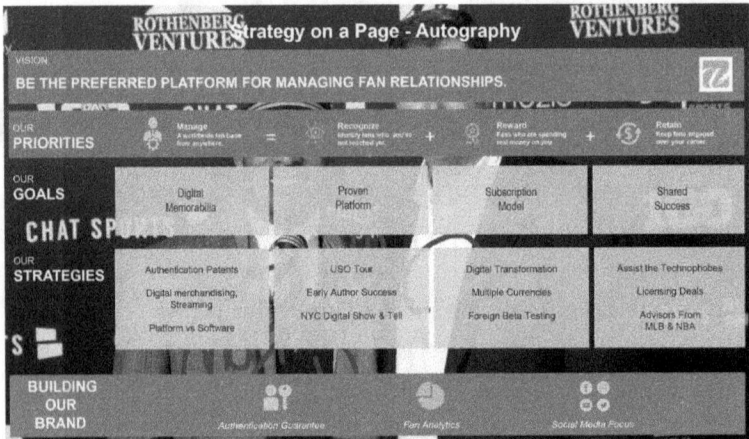

Figure 6.4 SOAP for Autography

It is pretty simple to figure out a SOAP for a start-up founder. Can anyone do the same for a young firm they're not a part of? Sure, let's look at SOAP for two of the GE Ventures portfolio companies I mentioned in Chapter 3. What would (my understanding of) Menlo Micro and Xometry look like in a Strategy-on-a-Page slide?

Menlo Microsystems

Menlo Microsystems' webpage says they're looking at a $5B opportunity in miniaturized electronic switch systems (Figure 6.5). The question here isn't where they're going—it might be easier to cite industries where they can't be useful—because that would be a short list. Anyone making anything electronic is a target for these guys. The sky's not the limit for them—they'll get to the new commercialized space industry soon enough.

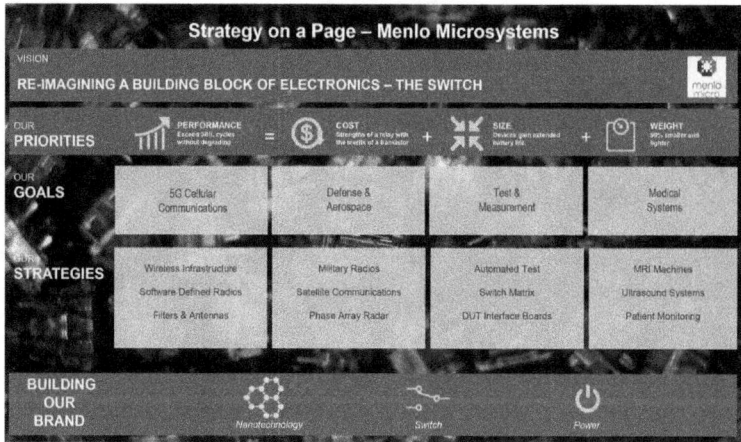

Figure 6.5 SOAP for Menlo Microsystems

Xometry

As the prior chapter suggests, despite their young age these folks have been able to make significant headway in multiple industries with some of the largest corporations in the world. The problem they are tackling is (1) significant and (2) lacks a front runner in the solution space. Xometry has a long runway ahead, a circumstance every founder dreams of (Figure 6.6).

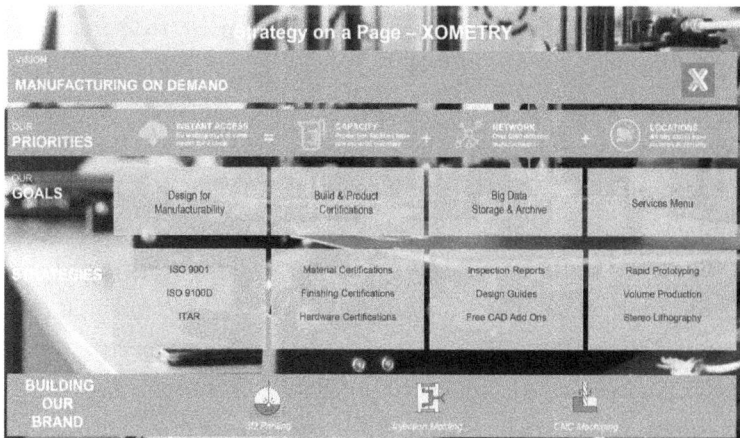

Figure 6.6 SOAP for Xometry

How about a start-up that successfully attracted customers who then became investors? Here is one (again, my interpretation, not theirs).

Rivian

An MIT engineer founded an electric pickup truck start-up that attracted Amazon first as a customer, then as an investor (Figure 6.7). Ford soon followed.

Figure 6.7 SOAP for Rivian

So, when approaching a corporation, be aware that the bigger the firm, the more entrenched in their "normal" ways of doing business they likely are. You're going to have to educate as much as advocate, so approach the discussions that way. Note I said discussions, *plural*—this is not a one-night stand. There will be multiple calls for the introduction, more calls and meetings for each stage of hand holding, and certainly more for any extended offers of partnership or investment. This is a marathon, not a hundred-yard dash. Plan accordingly.

But tools like SOAP make these discussions a little bit easier. For one, it forces founders to articulate clearly what their new ideas will mean. For large corporations, it gives them ways to look at a new concept dispassionately, evaluating what potential benefits it offers, or threatens if it is taken by a competitor, in a very straightforward manner.

With many start-up pitch events moving into hybrid modes of in person and online simultaneously, start-up founders and corporate innovation managers can "speed date" to find each other. While not perfect, it does offer the advantage of being a cost-effective way for companies to stay wired into various technology cities. This could be a good role for an intern, attending virtual start-up events worldwide looking for new technology investments.

They could check out the annual TechChill event in Riga, the capital city and center stage of Latvia's growing start-up scene. Budapest is another city that might surprise American managers with their entrepreneurial ecosystem. President Macron has advocated for start-up innovation in Paris via Station F and similar incubators,[3] while Berlin's start-up scene seeks to leverage Britain's EU exit to become Europe's new start-up capital.[4]

CHAPTER 7

Megatrends Driving the Start-Up Revolution

GE was one of the first manufacturers to acknowledge how digital technology was about to fundamentally change its business.[1] This was after an internal team researching Megatrends noted how Silicon Valley start-ups were gathering data from GE customers to develop new data-centric services in sectors such as aviation and energy to identify new revenue sources.

The impact of these changes can be seen with GE itself. In November 2021, it announced it was splitting up into three separate companies focusing on energy, health care, and aviation.[2] CEO Larry Culp told investors the split would allow each separated firm to have *greater focus, tailored capital allocation, and strategic flexibility to drive long-term growth and value.*

Within a single week, two other firms announced similar breakups: Toshiba and Johnson & Johnson (J&J).[3] Toshiba will similarly break into three separate firms, while J&J will simply split into halves. Their size, once the basis for economies of scale, is now a liability. Smaller and more nimble competitors are no longer nipping at their heels—they're sinking their disruptive teeth into the fat complacency of larger firms.

Three primary forces—technology, globalization, and demographics—are evolving in a succession of waves involving artificial intelligence, robotics, urban migration, aging populations, millennial workforces, and more.[4] To these I might add the pervasive use of sensors, cameras, and microphones that are fundamentally changing not simply user experiences (UX) but also how some of these systems will operate in the future.

These interacting waves stirred the field of behavioral economics to address challenges such as climate change and chronic disease, as digital platforms enable real-time and real-world behavior modification.[5]

This disruption is changing the way the world works faster than many large corporations can react. Businesses are responding to shifts that would have been unimaginable even a few years ago.[6]

Megatrends analysis suggests how legacy corporations can prepare for these changes. Oxford Dictionary defines Megatrends as *"An important shift in the progress of a society or of any other particular field or activity; any major movement."* I've outlined a dozen general Megatrends here and I suggest start-ups focus on no more than six that leaders believe can create the most stakeholder value in their planning for the future.

There is a wide variety of published material to wade through to determine which Megatrends are (a) important and (b) relevant from a start-up market opportunity perspective. In an increasingly global marketplace, no corporation wants to skew toward an exclusive nationality, ethnicity, or political preference. There are many issues that remain out of a corporation's control, and for these purposes, I'm limiting our interests to areas a company can act on in a timely manner.

This approach uses a technique called STEEPLE analysis.[7] This stands for Societal, Technological, Environmental, Economic, Political, and Legal/Ethical analysis (Figure 7.1).

I'll define these metrics as:

- *Societal*: Societies are being reshaped from the forces of global connectivity, remote work, and digital commerce. Paradoxically, as delivery times decrease for products between us diminishes, the perceptual distance between us grows. Much of the world will live longer lives, yet will also increasingly suffer from chronic diseases, requiring long-term medical monitoring and management.
- *Technological*: Starting with smartphones and moving to wearables, technology is no longer something intentionally sought out; it is constantly with us. Data availability and control is becoming a problem as control over the analysis of data, both personally and communally, is evading our grasp in ways we'd not intended. Long-term storage and authorization of raw data and finished analysis will require new understanding of its impact.

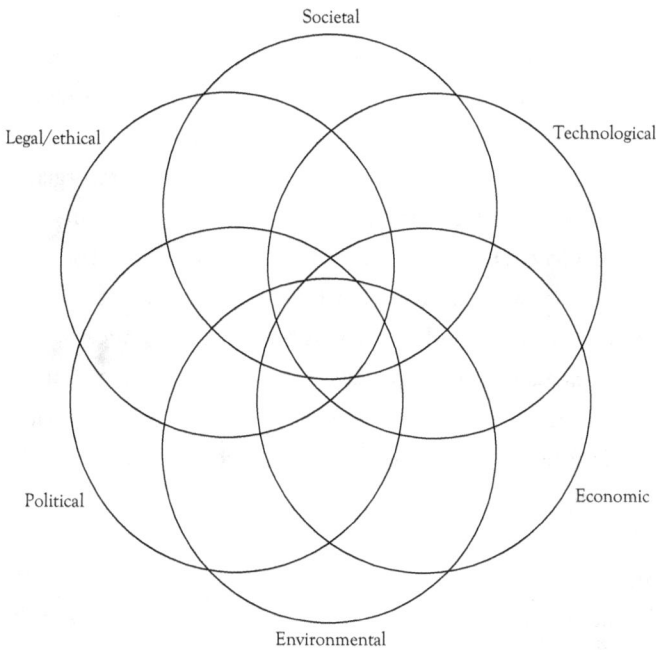

Figure 7.1 STEEPLE analysis

- *Environmental*: Climate change continues to be a political, technological, and social issue, perhaps more than a scientific one. Western wildfires and eastern hurricanes wreak havoc annually, while tornadoes and flooding devastate the nation's breadbasket. This is testing our energy infrastructure at a difficult point, as much of the nation's electrical grid is showing its age.
- *Economic*: Covid-19 drove a stake into the heart of "normal" economic activity. Working from home became the rule rather than the exception for those who had jobs. A "return to normal" has stalled as many lower wage employees hesitated to return to work, while higher paying jobs are seeing incredible turnover. A potential housing crisis is looming as sale and rental prices skyrocket despite the uncertainty over jobs.
- *Political*: Trust in government is at an all-time low, with both sides of the aisles pointing fingers. Unusual fractures have also emerged at the federal versus state (and local) levels,

as funding challenges, Covid responses, and unexpected migratory movements are challenging the ability of leaders to respond in consistent ways, driving an additional wedge between citizens and their elected officials.

- *Legal/Ethical*: Global regulations are taking on a new urgency, from taxes and tariffs to how to best respond to ransomware. Cyber criminals appear to operate with impunity, while nation-states take turns accusing each other of fostering global networks of professional hackers. Concerns over state-sponsored espionage are echoed by a perception that technology firms are similarly engaging in commercial espionage at the expense of citizen privacy and national governance.

Through a STEEPLE analysis, companies can identify a range of global trends affecting and being affected by a variety of pressures. For my theoretical corporation here I have racked-and-stacked these trends, noting points where common technologies are at play with several of them. One way to customize this wide-ranging analysis is to designate something a relevant Megatrend when it occurs at the intersection of three of these STEEPLE metrics. Every company should do its own analysis, but for our theoretical exercise, here is one possible result (Figure 7.2).

Changes in the world are affecting people's perception of value, and consequently their perception of how to value a corporation.[8] Successful providers are proactive in approaching customers with new service proposals and creative in articulating their capabilities to define new ways to add value and take the lead in redesigning their customer's value chain.

Properly managed, start-up companies can help a legacy corporation manage this unwieldy assortment better than, cheaper than, and faster than it can manage on its own. The core product line or service of the corporation (i.e., its cash cow) must continue, but many ancillary points of differentiation will continue to grow and evolve. The best metaphor for this is a baseball term: *bench depth*.

By having a varied array of start-up resources operating independently of the corporation itself, Boards and C-suite executives can have the resources to call up for these challenges as they emerge. Some may be

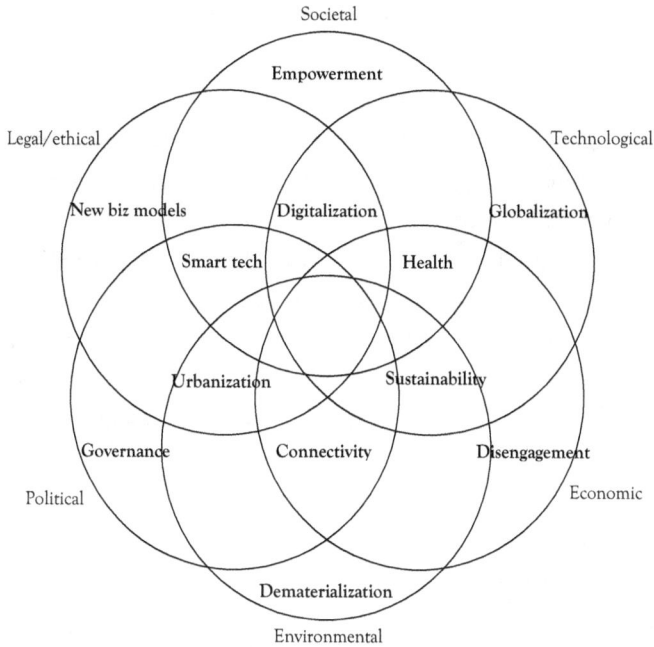

Societal

Empowerment

Legal/ethical

Technological

New biz models   Digitalization   Globalization

Smart tech   Health

Urbanization   Sustainability

Governance   Connectivity   Disengagement

Political   Economic

Dematerialization

Environmental

Figure 7.2 STEEPLE megatrends

"warming the bench" within the corporation itself, others may be in various double-A or triple-A "minor leagues" elsewhere, developing their new skills with talented staff and coaches.

Megatrend Definitions

In developing a Megatrends strategy, it is important that all stakeholders be on the same page (Figure 7.3). Again, for our exercise we'll define the Megatrends that offer opportunities and threats.

1. *Connectivity*: As the pandemic forced everyone to stay indoors, people took to the Internet to connect with family across the street and across the world. Instructed to maintain "social distance" even from those in their own household, video platforms such as Zoom and WebEx became lifelines to the elderly who were most at risk from the virus. School children attended class via Microsoft Teams to prevent disease transmission between households. At the same time, with

travel limited, streaming services delivered new content to seize a captive audience's attention.

2. *Dematerialization*: Older generations are increasingly adopting younger cohort's preferences for easily *accessing* a product or service versus directly *acquiring* or owning it. The proliferation of digital technology that created ride-sharing platforms such as Uber and Lyft are expanding into adjacent markets to deliver everything from toothpaste to televisions. Though trepidation remains over autonomous vehicles and drones, new investments are producing results. People are doing more (activity) with less (space), preferring to dedicate their financial resources to experiences and travel versus possessions.

3. *Digitalization*: Big data is no longer the exclusive purview of Silicon Valley's tech titans. Now, even the smallest of individual retailers is expected to have cutting-edge digital payment systems, state-of-the-art inventory management, and just-in-time product delivery. Competitive advantage has moved quickly to the online world in every day, real life activity. Payments between friends, from splitting a bar bill out to splitting a rent payment at home is increasingly done from smartphones rather than formal banking systems. Every transaction is likely also geo-tagged, providing a "where" to the "what."

4. *Disengagement*: At the same time smartphones are connecting more people than ever before, our face-to-face relationships have suffered. Deep connections on a personal level have been supplanted by likes, thumbs up, and forwards on social media. When not engaging with others, many millennials are absorbed into streaming music or binge-watching television to block out the real world. (The headphone industry grew 4–8 percent *annually* the past seven years.[9])

5. *Empowerment*: The power dynamic has tilted toward the individual over the group, and the greatest indicator of this is the movement toward a sharing economy. Finding ways for person "A" to use idle capacity of person "B" has expanded dramatically. Airbnb and other platform-based applications allow users to share a single asset across distance, culture, and time. Racial and ethnic movements are becoming increasingly common and spilling into the streets, sometimes leading to violence.

6. *Globalization*: Nationalism is an increasingly unwanted word in the United States, as more citizens identify as members of the global community than as Americans. Lack of enforcement on our southern border has morphed from a political crisis to a humanitarian one as hundreds of migrants cross the border daily now unimpeded. Children are being left on or near the U.S.-Mexico border by parents, creating all new pressures for a Customs and Immigration Enforcement bureau that was already under economic strain.

7. *Governance*: The 2016 American Presidential election continues to reverberate across the country, as does the ongoing legal and political fallout from the U.S. Capitol riots. Bipartisanship is a word thrown around quite a lot, but never quite followed through by leaders from either major political party. The United States clumsily withdrew from Afghanistan, which has reinvigorated the Taliban to fill the leadership vacuum.

8. *Health*: Predictive health care seeks to prevent future diseases rather than treat them after the fact. Smartphone applications and wearable devices are monitoring numerous data points that are analyzed by top research universities through cooperative data-sharing policies. While the population is aging, it is also leveraging remote health monitoring of individuals at scale, radically shifting how clinical research may be done in the very near future.

9. *New Business Models*: We are witnessing unprecedented monetization of data. The sharing economy spearheaded by Uber and Lyft has spread to interrupt other legacy industries in ways most of them never expected. Some of these operate outside the global SWIFT banking system, making them difficult for regulators to monitor. These systems also affect how and where people work, building the GIG economy in leaps and bounds.

10. *Remote Work*: Americans are on the move like never before. Escaping high taxes and real estate, traditional job-centric cities such as San Francisco and New York are witnessing an exodus of workers due to violence and rapidly rising murder rates. Now that work is no longer location-based people are leaving to find quality of life, thinking that when the pandemic is over, they can trade concrete and glass for cafes and grass. (In 1970, there were two megacities—populations

of over 10,000,000—these were Tokyo and New York. Today there are 23, a figure projected to grow to 41 by 2030.[10]) This is driving up home prices in many parts of the country, reducing inventory, which in turn drives up rental prices as well.

11. *Smart Technology*: More and more products are linked through the Internet, not just to share (our) data but also for (the device's) maintenance, software upgrades, and cybersecurity patches. This has outpaced the industry's ability to meet demand, creating unexpected chip shortages. It has been particularly problematic in the automotive industry, which is simultaneously trying to shift to electric vehicles (EVs) that will be orders of magnitude more connected than gas-powered cars ever were.

12. *Sustainability*: Renewed interest in sustainability has challenged numerous industries. Ocean plastics, long an academic problem, is now openly discussed by celebrities and music artists.[11] Interest in smart packaging has expanded from sensors and connectivity to full cycle cradle-to-grave policies. Additional investment in wind and solar technologies are trying to improve their energy storage capacities to use in nonpeak times. EVs are surging, compelled by Tesla's success, with multibillion dollar commitments by every major brand and state-sponsored investments from China.

Globalization and rising incomes in emerging nations may drive frugal innovation, which implies that services and products need not be of inferior quality but must be provided inexpensively. Successful advanced service providers are proactive in approaching customers with new proposals and creative in taking their own capabilities to the customer to define new ways to add value and take the lead in redesigning their customers value chain.[12]

Start-ups addressing this array of disruptive technologies may have much in common with corporate or divisional leaders desiring to prepare for the coming change. Every corporation should create their own STEEPLE matrix to identify and support the investments that are relevant in multiple categories. By reducing the larger megatrends list from 12 to 6, (those that touch multiple areas), companies can evaluate how

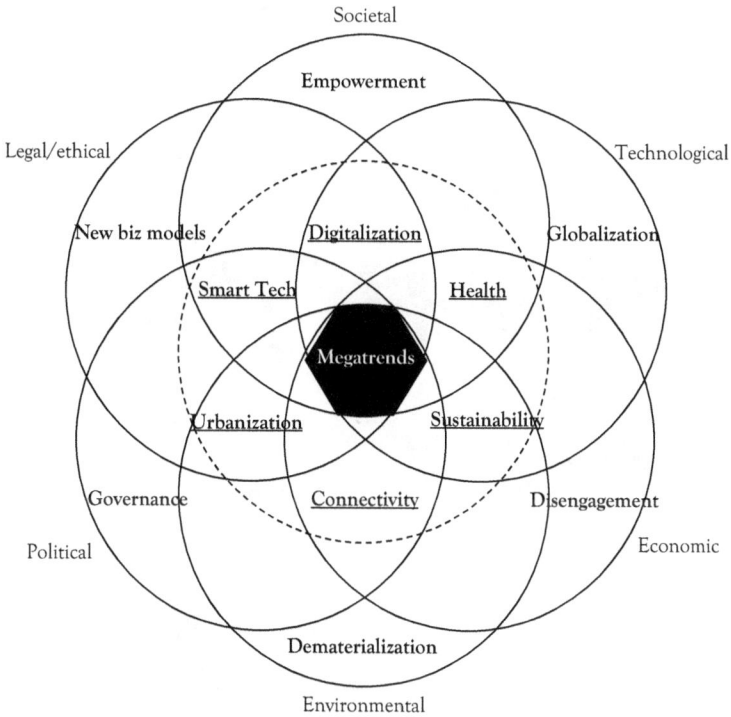

Figure 7.3 "Closest" megatrends

both the drivers of disruption and their technology investments align with this matrix.

There are likely start-up companies that would perfectly scratch a big corporation's itch in any of a number of these megatrend areas. Partnering, investing in, or acquiring new technologies around these areas can be significant public relations milestones as well, helping legacy corporations extend their goodwill into the future.

CHAPTER 8

Embracing Disruption

Peter Drucker once wrote *"Every single social and global issue of our day is a business opportunity in disguise."*[1] In evaluating which start-up technologies they want to assist and develop, corporations should take Drucker's message to heart, considering these opportunities wherever, and however, they may appear in the context of their future business interests.

It's best for every company to take a bottom-up approach, looking at specific innovations from customer, division, and industry perspectives—then roll those up the value chain based on demand and opportunity. Many of these drivers are global, reflective of how technology has morphed with innovations retooled, repackaged, and reintroduced under different titles.

Other drivers are limited to specific businesses or industries based on technology platforms, national regulations, cultural norms, or regional limitations. For example, products may need to be differentiated for particular markets even though they come from the same factory. This *"mass customization"* is increasingly common, as regulatory and cultural influences seem to be in constant flux.

Understanding this, every company wants to leverage their technology investments to get the maximum return possible given the time and resource limitations they face. Customers want the latest and greatest technology but demand minimal cost. These opposing forces mean big corporations must always be looking to improve efficiencies. Start-ups can help them do this.

We begin with the drivers—the individual innovations, inventions, and technologies that come from academics, garage-based innovators, and yes, even our competitors. A quick news search reveals a wide array of potential technology investment areas any company might want to work within. These can include (in no order):

- *Amazonization*
- 5G wireless
- Artificial intelligence
- A/R and V/R
- The Internet of Things (IOT)

- Blockchain
- Social media
- Electric vehicles
- Cloud data regulations
- Ransomware attacks

Every Board of Directors will gauge these and other pressures in short-, mid-, and long-term time horizons, also (hopefully) asking their own executive staff which ones are most pressing for senior leadership to consider. These factors are then viewed through the lens of how the company makes technology investment decisions.

Like the drivers themselves, these investments are sometimes complimentary. Others may be in competition. As they are corporate investments, companies want to squeeze as much knowledge out of them as possible to avoid duplicating work by different groups, while still advertising (promoting, rewarding) successes so that others can also benefit.

*Mega*trends are built by the confluence of individually successful trends that compete and coalesce as they build. In Chapter 1, I noted the difference between market intelligence and market strategy. If you're going to be prepared to adjust your strategy (*ahem, pivot*) to changing market conditions, you'd better know what those conditions are. That means market intelligence.

Volumes have been written about the intelligence cycle and what all is involved in monitoring the marketplace. For our start-up interests here let's stick to the basics of that cycle—those are (1) collection, (2) analysis, (3) reporting, and (4) planning.

- *Collection*: A funnel is really the right way to characterize collection because it's coming in from everywhere. Human sources, published reports, competitor's patent filings, Wall Street investment analysis, and much more.
- *Analysis*: Drinking from the information collection firehose without drowning in meaningless facts can be challenging.

Having good data analysts is tremendously important in separating the important from the irrelevant.

- *Reporting*: Once that analysis is done it has to be relayed to the decision maker. Knowing your audience is key here. How do they like information—the 10,000-foot view or the gory details? That is two very different types of reporting.
- *Planning*: Once leaders understand the analysis they must act. What changes does the information elicit? If nothing changes, the report that was delivered was NOT intelligence. It was simply data. If there's no action, there was no intelligence.

This might seem like a military operation, and yes, I did spend some time in that world. But what I learned was that the underlying leadership skill is the same. It is decision making.

Whether you're the current resident of 1600 Pennsylvania Avenue, a ground commander taking a hill, or an entrepreneur disrupting a market, the primary job is the same: Can you make decisions quickly, with imperfect information, under incredible time pressure? If not, you've no business being in the lead role, because that is all you have to look forward to.

No matter the task, this is what it all boils down to. Coat and tie, dress uniform, or laptop bag over your shoulder—leading a small team into the unknown is very nerve-wracking. You will be wrong from time to time. Can you live with that?

Are young men and women going to die from your decision making? No, not likely. But their careers, their family's stability, and surely your own mental health hang in the balance. Don't underestimate just how difficult the top job can be. It's not all option grants and celebrations. There are many potential low points too. Things you didn't anticipate, didn't expect the competition to challenge, or didn't realize the market had already decided on.

That is what all this intelligence gathering and analysis provides. It gives you some warning. It allows you to see trends developing early enough that you can take action to address them before anyone else does. It gives you a competitive advantage in that you are not caught off guard.

Individual trends break through these areas and often end up as force multipliers. Individually they may have only a marginal affect, but together they can build, evolving and changing as they grow, and become overarching megatrends.

So for your corporation, consider three division areas and how they can use this analysis to define what sorts of start-up innovations they might want. This might also help them decide—should these be our own intrapreneurs or outside start-ups? Does the company want to partner with established entities or are there new start-ups being launched that the company wants to seed fund (or more)?

Health

As noted, health care is seeing an enormous shift as (1) the population ages, (2) there is a 20-year shortage on health care labor, and (3) chronic disease management is emerging as a primary factor in results-based health care. I can envision a corporation's interests in health care in the following ways, via <u>Drivers</u>, *Investments*, and **Trends** (Figure 8.1).

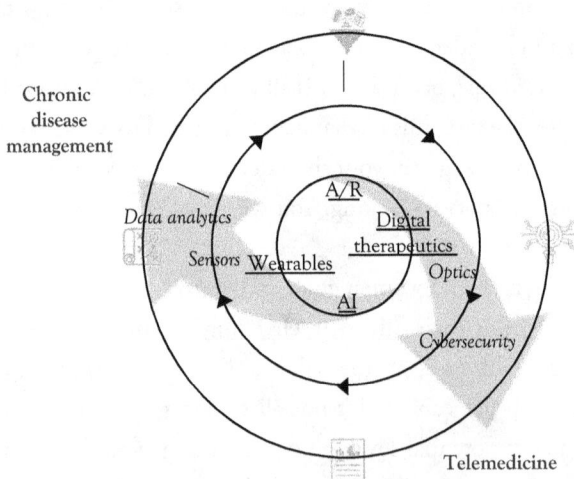

Figure 8.1 Health care megatrend

- <u>Augmented Reality</u> is changing how doctors treat patients from diagnosis to surgery. As hardware costs come down, these systems will become even more popular.
- <u>Digital Therapeutics</u> utilize online health technology to treat a medical or psychological condition. One example could be a digital management program for type II diabetes.[2]

- *Optics* have vastly improved smartphone use, and software will apply advanced medical imagery to smartphone cameras in radically new ways.
- *Cybersecurity* will ensure patient authentication and health care professional authority for who can access health data, responding to the #1 hacking target: Health care.[3]
- **Telemedicine** will enable more patients to be treated at home versus going to a health care office. I expect widespread acceptance of telemedicine by private sector and government insurance providers as a far less expensive alternative.

Telemedicine is primarily a result of data transmitted elsewhere for processing. Prior to the Covid-19 pandemic, studies in 2018 showed the average cost to insurers for a telemedicine consultation is $45, compared to a $120 in-office visit.[4] I suspect that figure has dropped even further now.

Sustainability

This megatrend has been growing for years. While packaging is likely seeing the most industrywide attention being paid to sustainability, it is nonetheless affecting all our businesses in one way or another. One set of Drivers, *Investments*, and **Trends** I can see here include the following (Figure 8.2):

- The Sharing Economy, as the population ages, fewer young people are interested in owning cars; a change the industry is starting to recognize.
- Mobile Payments are replacing bank branches and even cash itself as young people shun mainstream financial institutions.[5]
- *Wireless* systems are making transactions fast and painless. From "*Grab and Go*" Amazon stores to Apple Pay's acceptance at restaurants, the term "cash register" is outdated.
- *Audio/Acoustics* now means you can simply order out loud and a smart device will understand what you said. Chinese

Autonomous cars

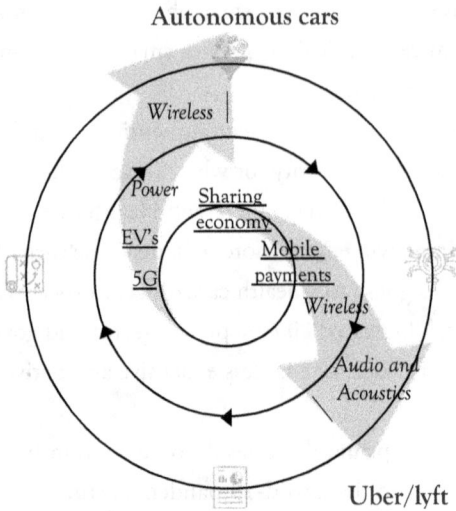

Figure 8.2 Sustainability megatrend

e-commerce giant Alibaba recently released voice controls for automobiles to search for restaurants and order takeout.[6]

- **Uber/Lyft** are making gains on older populations, particularly for medical visits. For younger buyers, one Los Angeles real estate developer replaced parking spaces with ride-sharing memberships for his condos.[7]

Uber and Lyft are not only results of technology but they are also platforms for it. Autonomous vehicles (itself another trend) are now an area of intense focus by both firms, potentially putting their own drivers out of work in a few years.

Digitalization

What isn't being digitized these days? From connected appliances in the home, to connected pets walking around the home, everything is linked. I doubt everyone has completely considered how much all the data coming from these connected devices are changing the world around us. Here I see a different series of <u>Drivers</u>, *Investments*, and **Trends** (Figure 8.3):

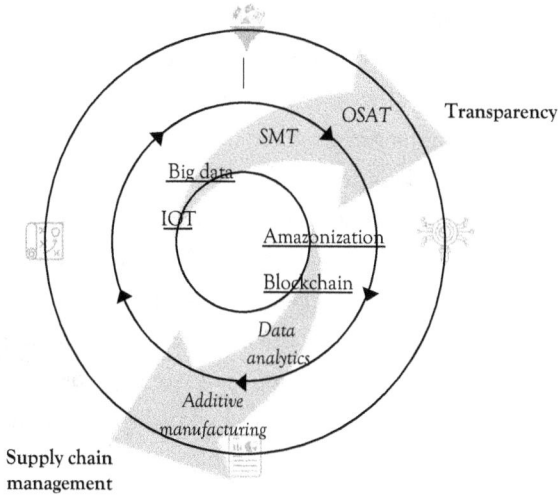

Figure 8.3 Digitalization megatrend

- <u>Amazonization</u> from e-commerce giant to the number two search engine and soon to be the number three digital advertising platform.
- <u>Blockchain</u> may evolve from an overhyped anticounterfeiting tool and become a required infrastructure feature for many transactions.
- *Data Analytics* is becoming a unique differentiator for companies as the "war for talent" continues to build.[8]
- *Additive Manufacturing* is moving beyond prototyping and product development to a true production-scale economic model.
- **Supply Chain Management** will become an essential partner to all companies, not just manufacturers, tracking digital as well as physical assets.

Supply Chain Management is proving that without robust information management systems, it will be impossible to be a viable business in the very near future. I noted this in a prior chapter on Amazon's move to Nashville with its abundance of college graduates in computer science and data analytics. IT, once relegated as a back-office function, is quickly emerging as a competitive differentiator across all industries.

For all Megatrends, there are a variety of component trends rising and falling. Some Megatrends see various trends building up in diverse data-centric ways. Others may see concentration in only one or two areas. Globally focused corporations see these trends building across divisions. What they must try to do is manage those pressures.

If every compounding **Trend** within Sustainability were displayed the image would be impossible to make out, so I've limited each display to two (Figure 8.4). For the three Megatrends cited previously, each business will see these pressures compounded in different ways. Within Sustainability for instance, *Wireless* as a driver may come up a couple of times.

Hopefully, by the nature of the way a company pursues its research investments, it can leverage the staff, equipment, and other resources at its disposal to maximize the benefits it can use on *Wireless* to satisfy multiple needs within the Sustainability Megatrend. Lessons learned, problems averted, and expenses avoided are but three of these benefits.

Other benefits may span the enterprise geographically and divisionally. Technology managers from very different businesses should compare notes about what works and what doesn't. Here, *Data Analytics* is a need that corporate managers in separate divisions share in common. With *Wireless*, the need is for different customers within the same division. Start-up companies specializing on such dissimilar shared-needs areas can free up corporate resources, outsourcing development so it is addressed quicker than can be done internally.

In actuality of course, this is not a linear process. Individual driver/disruptors do not fit nicely one-to-one into a single investment category. Life is not unsullied and neither is business. The many disruptors a corporation faces are complex as well as complicated. They bounce off each other, as force multipliers as well as power disablements. As a result, each Megatrend is a combination of numerous underlying trends; each contributes in its own way and on its own timeline. This is what makes them MEGA.

Every company must act upon these many trends, and subsequent Megatrends, in their own way. Interpretations will be different, strategies will vary, and certainly outcomes will be individually unique. Some opportunities will be lost, but in other cases, serious threats will

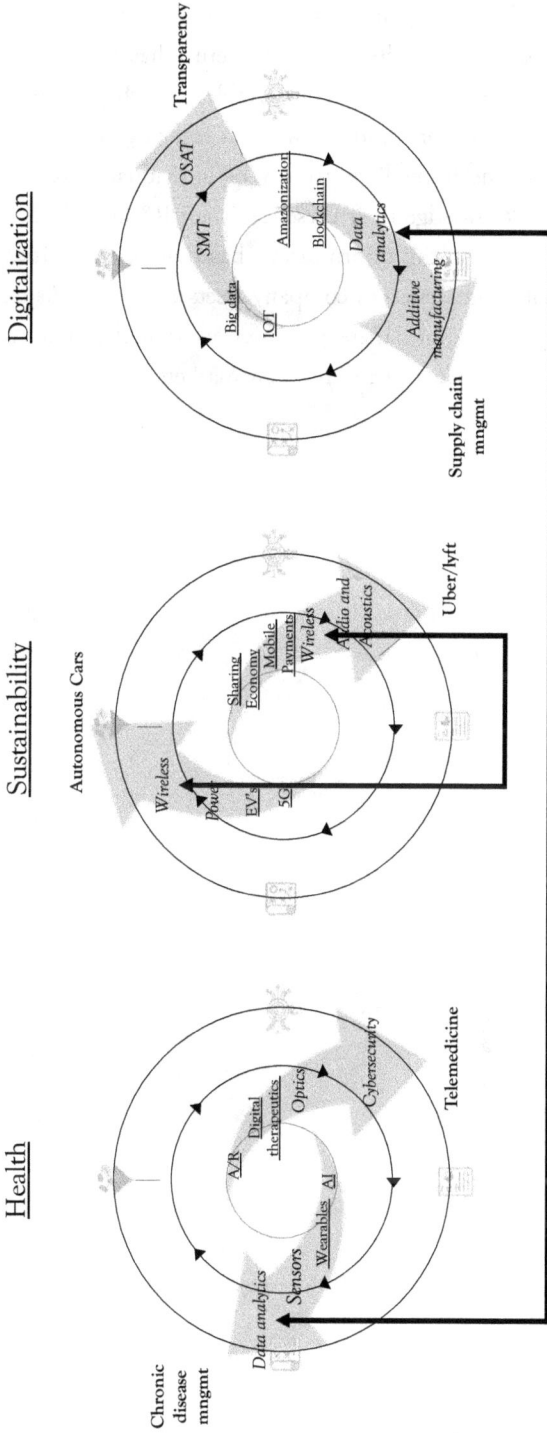

Figure 8.4 Common interests across megatrends

be avoided. Unfortunately, many times those can only be properly and completely measured after the point of no return has passed.

Corporate leaders must get comfortable that they have addressed the drivers and disruptors head on, without fear or favor. They may not always agree on the immediate priority of individual drivers, but they must at least acknowledge their presence. Their R&D and other investments hopefully reflect this prioritization, based on opportunities for new revenue as well as protection of company assets and brand. As trends rise and fall, they must adjust these priorities accordingly, in concert with customers as they move forward into new markets.

CHAPTER 9

Humans Are the Resources

I detailed Intel Corporation's success at raising money with a very simple, three-paragraph business plan. The fact that it was successful was in no way meant to suggest the fundraising process was simple. It wasn't. Quite the contrary in fact.

Intel offered equity positions, (investment opportunities), to a range of big-name brand companies in the technology space. Litton, Borg Warner, Ford, Motorola, NCR, General Mills, McGraw Electric, Magnavox, and Sylvania are among the three dozen firms who declined to invest. Intel hasn't forgotten—despite some recent setbacks, the company still has plenty of brand swagger and a bit of a chip on its shoulder. Culturally, they still remember what it was like to be a young firm. Put another way, Intel is Tom Brady!

In a July 2021 speech accepting his championship ring for Super Bowl 55, Brady talked not about his success, but rather about other team's doubts.[1] How leaders in other NFL organizations questioned his abilities and resolve. When he was originally drafted, Tom was a sixth-round pick; one hundred and ninety-ninth overall. How many of those teams don't slap their foreheads every year recalling the day they *passed over Tom Brady*? That should be tattooed on the forehead of every scout and manager involved.

He's never forgotten it. It burns him, fuels him, to this day. And the doubt remains! When he left the Patriots, hailed as the GOAT (Greatest of All Time), another team still refused to hire him![2] He makes a point of rubbing it in the face of this team he will not publicly name. But again, it fuels him!

(Regret can be a very painful lesson. Former Atari CEO Nolan Bushnell lightheartedly bemoans his decision to ***not*** acquire 30 percent of Apple Computer.[3] His former employee Steve Jobs offered one-third of the then start-up for $50,000. Jobs and Steve Wozniak's minimally viable product—the Apple 1—was built from borrowed Atari computer parts! The value of that one-third equity position would be in the billions now.)

Intel Corporation, still smarting from all the companies that didn't believe in them, has not made this same mistake. Their venture capital team has invested in 1,500 start-up companies in and out of Silicon Valley.[4] Over 700 of these have already realized a payoff from an IPO or acquisition. Did Intel do it for the financial return? I think not. Their sterling reputation simply shines a bit brighter when hundreds of other technology thought leaders speak so reverently of them.

That is brand management!

Will all the start-ups succeed? Of course not—that's not the point. Founders who fail will lick their wounds, try to fit their employees into other nearby companies, and take some time to figure out their next move. Most will eventually dust themselves off, update their resume, and try it all over again. Failure doesn't define an entrepreneur. Repeatedly trying, even if it takes years, does!

Haloid Photographic provides a great example of this approach. After taking over as CEO from his father, 40-year-old Joseph C. Wilson licensed a new dry photocopying process from a young inventor named Chester Carlson.[5] Wilson spent 10 percent of the company's earnings to acquire the technology and a decade to commercialize it. They even coined a word, "xerography," to describe the process.

As you might have guessed that company eventually changed its name to Xerox, and completely crushed its crosstown rival Kodak. There were no doubt times during the intervening years when shareholders, employees, and possibly even Wilson himself doubted his resolve. But today, Xerox has a market cap of just under $5B, over seven times the value of Kodak, who emerged from bankruptcy in 2013.[6]

Apples and oranges? No, not really. Kodak invented the digital camera. Imagine if they had chosen **not** to quash the 15 years of R&D and considerable funds they'd invested in that technology. What if they instead commercialized it like their development team wanted to? Where would they be now? Can you imagine Kodak as the brains, brawn, or brand behind Snap, Instagram, or Tik Tok? The product developers who toiled away for a decade only to get benched no doubt can!

Some would argue a company cannot successfully pivot from its original business. I say that is complete nonsense. It is a choice, like anything else. It takes leadership, confidence, and a fair amount of will. But it can be done. It is done every day. In fact many companies we know today began as something else completely:

- Wrigley started out as a soap company that gave away free baking powder. It pivoted to a baking powder company that gave away gum. Then it pivoted again to confectionaries.
- Avon began as a bookseller who attracted buyers with perfume samples, pivoting to a cosmetics company.
- Suzuki began as builder of looms for silk weaving before pivoting to motorcycles and other small-motor machines.
- Shopify was a snowboard store called Snowdevil before pivoting to focus on e-commerce.

Abbott Laboratories Chairman Albert White told *The Wall Street Journal* companies must *"be their own activist investor."*[7] While White was referring to spinoffs of large divisions or subsidiaries as stand-alone firms, I think the same can be said of start-ups that don't fit the company's current business.

If corporations aren't embarking on new technologies, you can be assured current competitors, or a new one you've never heard of, is certainly doing so with the intent of taking away some of your market share. Spinoffs, start-up acquisitions, and venture capital shops allow companies to iterate in low-risk, low-cost ways that maximize benefits to all stakeholders (Figure 9.1).

Microsoft is seeking start-up partnerships in its competition against Amazon.[8] If this isn't a Harvard Business School case already, I encourage someone to write one. One of the biggest, most successful software companies on earth, trying to compete against the de facto e-commerce behemoth, is soliciting help from start-ups. New companies, trying new things, many of whom will fail—this is who Microsoft wants to partner with.

Why are they doing this? They are looking for new business opportunities. They are (rightfully) unsatisfied with *"the way we've always done*

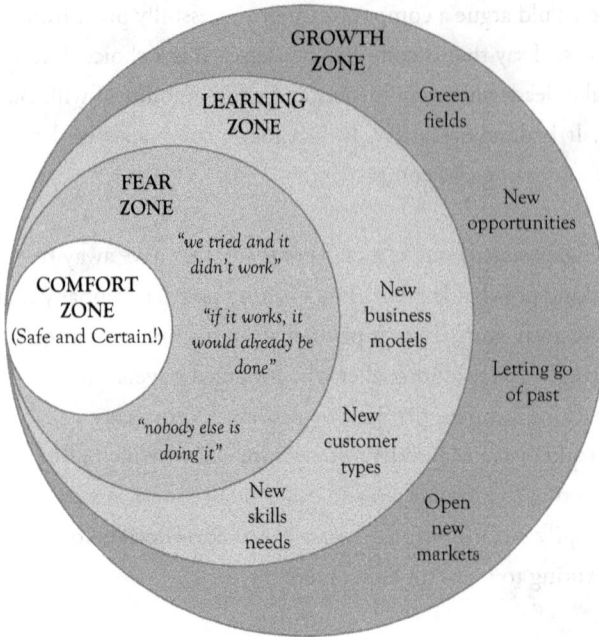

Figure 9.1 Comfort zone to growth zone

it" and are looking for ways nobody has ever done before. If that means they move away from legacy businesses, so be it. Microsoft Office was originally a downloaded software product. Now, Microsoft 365 is a sub-scription service. So despite their size, the Seattle giant is boldly pushing the boundaries of change.

They're not alone. Tesla created a $199/month subscription service for an advanced version of its signature driver's assistance feature. Morgan Stanley said in a research note the value of that subscription service alone could eventually exceed the value of selling Tesla cars.[9] That value can come from unexpected places. Airlines including Delta, American, and United have issued bonds or other debt instruments to raise money. But rather than put up their planes, they used their (intangible) loyalty programs as collateral.[10]

General Electric recently sold off its lightbulb business.[11] Let me say that again—it sold off *its lightbulb business*! Thomas Edison's icon for innovation used in every Power Point deck and GE no longer owns it. Why? Because they've made a conscious decision it's not the future of their company.

GOATing Them On

Referring again to Tampa Bay quarterback Tom Brady, much has been made of his age. The legendary athlete turns 45 this year, a time when most quarterbacks are laying back on their couches watching Sunday football with the rest of us. He's showing that age does not define ability. Many start-ups' founders have done the same.

Robert Noyce and Gordon Moore were over 35 when they approached Arthur Rock for help to launch Intel Corporation. They are hardly alone however, as "older" founders are now increasingly common. Pandora, Zynga, and Zipcar were all founded by entrepreneurs over the age of 35. Despite the traditional VC myth of founders dropping out of college to do a start-up in their garage, older founders, (including many corporate employees), bring a lot to the table.

In 2018, four researchers published their analysis of Census Bureau data that showed the average age of a start-up entrepreneur was actually 42.[12] They retabulated their results to eliminate unscalable entities like dry cleaners and restaurants, and refined it further to firms with at least one patent, had received venture capital investment, or were in industries with high Science, Technology, Engineering and Math (STEM) job counts. There the average age was 45. They also found that these older entrepreneurs had a substantially higher success rate than younger ones. To what did they attribute this success? *Business experience!*

I'm betting most of that experience came from corporate America. Older entrepreneurs have extensive industry relationships, contacts built over decades of conferences, trade shows, and seminars. They know people, *smart people*, like-minded people in their industries who can help them build a new business. Young entrepreneurs often don't have this support system network, so be mindful of long-time employees looking to break out into something new. They are now getting some help from outside organizations.

Venture Out is a new start-up program in Seattle that specializes in helping corporate employees leave to build their own start-ups.[13] What does that mean? It means their business model is to take away your corporation's employees, (you know, that "*most important asset*" HR people are always yammering about). For corporate employees stuck with archaic business models, sociopathic leadership, or arduous golden handcuffs, this is their Start-up of Liberty beacon!

Some companies get it though, and even with all the advantages that come with funding and personnel resources, many start-ups still fail. This book started out addressing that issue and I'm deliberately returning to that point as we near the end. You can't be afraid to fail!

Early in its history, Apple spun out a start-up called General Magic. Coming off the successful launch of the Macintosh computer, the team had a mission to build the "next big thing." General Magic did just that. But like the dragonfly drones I opened with, it was a successful failure. General Magic closed after their product development times grossly missed their mark. They had issues incorporating software and hardware together, and certainly missed out on what their product should cost versus others in the marketplace.

But General Magic may be the most successful failed start-up in history.

The talent within this one small firm is legendary in Silicon Valley to this day.[14] General Magic alumni who became start-up creators is a who's who of technology thought leadership, including the founders of Ebay, LinkedIn, and Android. A former CTO of the United States, Megan Smith, hired by President Barak Obama in 2014, was also a General Magic alumnus.[15]

Many other employees went back into Apple itself, such as Tony Fadell, (iPad and iPhone). A few remain there now, including VP of Engineering Kevin Lynch, (iWatch and very recently, Apple Car).[16] What does this tell you? Apple is savvy enough to recognize smart people, wise enough to bring them into the fold, and mature enough to not blame them for perceived past "mistakes." If only every company was so shrewd.

But if Apple "failed" with a spinoff like General Magic, why should anyone else think they can do it better? Let me ask you this—does anyone really think Apple *failed* by spinning General Magic out? Making mistakes is not failing—that is living. Companies are staffed by humans who always have and always will make mistakes.

Marc Porat, the CEO of General Magic, imagined a handheld device that could send and receive e-mail, store digital gift cards, and keep your calendar handy. He sketched out the concept of the smartphone

15 years before the iPhone was created! He was a creative visionary, and just like Steve Jobs, it cost him his job. (And like Steve Jobs, he turned out to be right.)

The key thing I would point out is that Apple did not have a formal incubator or accelerator program back in those days. Most companies didn't, even in Silicon Valley. The corporate incubator was an unknown concept at the time. But now it has evolved, morphed, spinning off a separate venture capital concept for funding as well. These are models every company should, and quite frankly, must adopt if they're going to succeed long term.

Was the absence of corporate oversight instrumental to both the success of General Magic's innovation *and* the reason for its eventual collapse? Probably so, but I think every single employee they had would sign up to do it all over again given the opportunity. These are the people who want to change the world and they're going to take their shot with or without a legacy corporation's help. You should prefer it be with you.

The more employees you have, the higher the odds that one or more of them are going to create a significant new business concept. Do you care if that enterprise is in your current industry? No, you should only care that your corporation can get a small sliver of that new accomplishment. That sliver might allow you to fund new R&D, new products, or explore new service areas you'd otherwise not be able to investigate. It's reward money for a risk, perhaps taken years ago, that can be plowed right back into other opportunities with other employees and their start-up concepts.

Imagine where you'll be in a couple of years.

CHAPTER 10

Actors in a Network

I've mentioned networks a couple of times. Distribution networks as a form of intellectual property (IP); expert networks that an incubator can provide; supplier networks a corporation typically has; and even the industry network of peers an older entrepreneur has that younger employees might not.

A company, be it a start-up or a multinational corporation, is also a network. As a thing it is largely conceptual in nature; a complex system of connected individuals that exists purely by will and legal agreement. That is both its strength and its weakness, as such networks are difficult to create but relatively simple to copy. Let me show you what I mean.

Television executives are a superstitious lot. They don't like risks. I'm not talking about jaywalking on Lexington Avenue, (which they all do). I'm talking about sinking millions of dollars, surrendering an expensive timeslot, and hiring unknown actors to play out a script written by some random screenwriter.

When those kinds of investments fail, it's the sort of thing that banishes a network big wig to a public broadcasting station in rural Nebraska. They prefer to stick with things they know will work. *They hate failure!* Witness the ongoing saga in finding a replacement for the late Alex Trebeck, host of the long-running game show *Jeopardy*. This is one of the most valuable television franchises in history, generating over $100M *in profits* every year.[1]

Network executives have been trying out a wide array of replacement hosts including quarterback Aaron Rogers, newscaster Anderson Cooper, and popular Star Trek alumni Levar Burton.[2] These "tryouts" went on for months as analysts sift through the ratings numbers to make sure they get it right.

Yet they managed to snatch defeat from the jaws of victory. Executive Producer Mike Richards was named the new host and the recriminations began almost immediately. It wasn't long before a deleted Tweet came back to haunt him, and he was summarily removed from the position.[3]

Game shows, comedies, dramas, and procedurals all have a specific rhythm, a model of what makes them resonate with an audience. Television executives spend a lot of money on market intelligence, so they know their target audiences. They know the audience's ages, incomes, locations, hobbies, and preferred brands, their music tastes and favorite movies. By knowing these attributes, television executives approve new programs that will be popular to the largest potential market.

Let's assume for a moment I'm a television executive tasked with building a half-hour comedy show. I'm developing a sitcom and I need to figure out what I'm going to offer. This will be a primetime show, so I must go easy on the sexual innuendo and strong language. That's more late night than family hour. Ditto for any nudity—anything you can't see on the beach should go to HBO instead. So, what am I looking to achieve?

New television shows are, essentially, start-up companies. It's a new concept, produced by a show runner that likely has some history in Hollywood and at least tacit knowledge of how the industry works. They'll pull together a few associates and hash out an idea for a new show—the same process start-up founders follow! The assembled cast, crew, and management don't always know each other at first, though there might be a few existing relationships here and there. So let's assume I've done that too!

I've sketched out a simple cast of characters for my situation comedy. Rather than one or two known personalities, I'm going to build an ensemble of newcomer actors that don't have a lot of baggage from a failed previous show. Here's what I have in mind:

- A very attractive and sweet, but mentally quite dense and untalented wanna-be actor.
- An obsessive-compulsive neat freak with a Mommy complex; someone whose career has benefited from a long-standing absence of a significant other.
- A classic geek, but with a Shakespeareanly dysfunctional childhood, one who uses sarcasm masked as humor as a defense mechanism.

- An opposing gender-parent obsessive with no self-confidence; a complete slave to outward appearances.
- An intelligent and successful professional who is socially incompetent; but wants someone to love (and to be loved) more than anything.
- A cultural outsider, struggling to fit into the other's world; their childlike innocence means they often miss the joke.

On the surface this appears as a random group of characters that would not normally be considered a "hot prospect" for television. Yet this was the number one comedy on broadcast television for a decade. This is *The Big Bang Theory*.

In the aforementioned order that is Penny, Sheldon, Leonard, Howard, Amy, and Raj. Launched by CBS in the fall of 2007, it took the market a season or two to get the joke. But once they did, the show was off to the races. *The Big Bang Theory*, (or *TBBT*), centers around four physicists and their girlfriends.

Penny (played by Kaley Cuoco) is an aspiring actress who moves in across the hall from Dr. Sheldon Cooper (played by Jim Parsons) and his roommate Dr. Leonard Hofstadter (Johnny Galecki). They work at Caltech in Pasadena, California, where they do work on theoretical and applied physics.

Dr. Cooper's girlfriend is neurobiologist Dr. Amy Farrah Fowler (Mayim Bialik). They have two close colleagues who frequently drop by the apartment: NASA engineering wizard Howard Wolowitz (Simon Helberg) and astronomer Dr. Rajesh Koothrappali (Kunal Nayyar).

In the character headshots first released by CBS, (note these are *character* depictions, not actor headshots), they appear innocuous enough. All the actors had some successes that brought them to this point, but only Mayim Bialik was really a "household name."

She was a former child actor, playing the lead role in the series *Blossom* for five seasons on NBC before taking a break to go to college, earning a PhD in Neuroscience. (Yes, an actor with a real PhD in Neuroscience plays a character with a PhD in Neuroscience in a television comedy. Who said Hollywood doesn't have a sense of humor?)

To understand why *TBBT* works, (and why replacing Alex Trebeck has taken so very long), you must appreciate two fundamental axioms of broadcast television (Figure 10.1):

1. Sponsors deliver programs to an audience.
2. Programs deliver audiences to a sponsor.

These two critical dynamics must be aligned. If not, a sponsor has paid for advertising on a show nobody watches, or the audience watching has no interest in the product being pitched. This is a recipe for disaster, one that has been repeated numerous times.

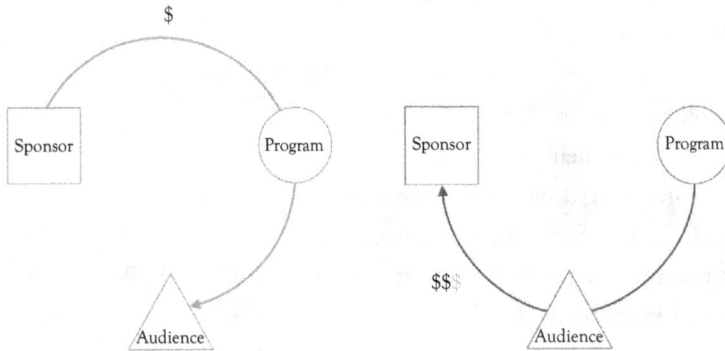

Figure 10.1 Broadcast TV model

But it's not just broadcast television. The same model is equally true for subscription channels (HBO and Showtime), streaming channels, (Apple + and Amazon Prime), and just about any other type of entertainment that is created and distributed to a potential market. It's why NETFLIX is now exploring a subscription version *with* advertising.[4] Money must be put up to back these new, unproven projects.

This is the same model for investors listening to start-up pitches. Corporate and venture investors are managing an identical process. They must make sure these two dynamics are in similar harmony:

1. Investors deliver start-ups to a market.
2. Start-ups deliver markets to investors.

When television programs are pitched, the target audience (that *market* in Keith Olsen's vernacular earlier) is the overarching factor (Figure 10.2). The same is true for anyone considering a start-up funding opportunity. Can the start-up deliver on that market potential with the founders (actors) as currently presented?

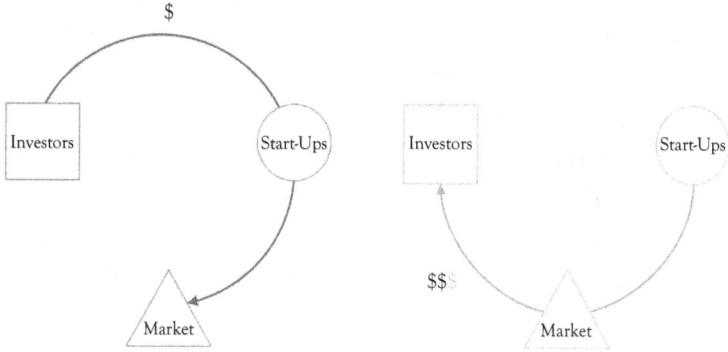

Figure 10.2 Similar start-up model

As a wise man once said, *"it's the same old thing, just a different crowd doing it."* In this case, it is corporate or VC investors evaluating how long it will take to see results and how much will there be? The very same questions producers ask when they evaluate where to spend their time and money.

The Big Bang Was No Theory

Different audiences prefer different types of programming. To engage the demographics they want (that also fit their other programs so they can cross-sell), television executives conduct a competitive analysis to determine the types of shows they should develop.

I want to produce a comedy. So, I'll create one that fits the demographic I want to advertise products for a market that has the disposable income to spend on those products and will tune in faithfully and repetitively for my show.

In a competitive analysis, executives consider what type of show was attractive to that audience in the past, that locked in the desired advertisers, and drove a "long tail" of ad revenues through syndicated reruns that go on for years.

They employ a technique called *Role Equivalence*, presenting the same role in a different context. So let's consider the characters I mentioned before. In my theoretical television executive persona I didn't simply make them up. I copied them from a successful show that existed previously. That's common in business—copying what you know works.

In this case, I mirrored those characters from a show that ran two decades ago with another broadcaster. A show called *Friends*. Let's recall those casting assignments:

A very attractive and sweet, but mentally quite dense and untalented wanna-be actor.

- Joey Tribiani (played by Matt LeBlanc), where a frequent show phrase was, "*It's a good thing you're pretty.*"

An obsessive-compulsive neat freak with a Mommy complex; whose career has benefited from the absence of a significant other.

- Monica Gellar (played by Courtney Cox). Monica was fat as a teenager until getting her eating under control—remember the "fat suit" episodes?

Classic geek with a Shakespeareanly dysfunctional childhood; uses sarcasm masked as humor for a defense mechanism.

- Chandler Bing (played by Mathew Perry). Chandler's father had a sex change late in life, (a role played with true comedic genius by Lauren Hutton).

Opposing gender-parent obsessive with no self-confidence; a complete slave to outward appearances.

- Rachel Green (played by Jennifer Aniston). Paradoxically, both Aniston and Simon Helberg have their appearances to thank as much as their talents for winning these roles.

Intelligent and successful professional, but socially incompetent; wants someone to love (and to be loved) more than anything.

- Dr. Ross Geller (played by David Schwimmer). His ex-wife decided, after their son was born, that she was a lesbian and divorced him.

A cultural outsider struggling to fit into the other's world; their childlike innocence means they often miss the joke.

- Phoebe Buffay (played by Lisa Kudrow). A street-performing musician/philosopher who adopts the five stereotypical Manhattan yuppies.

Side by side the character head shots show the obviousness of their similarities. Penny and Joey (the two would-be actors) are aloof; Sheldon and Monica are pensive, Leonard and Chandler look anxious, Howard and Rachael belie their lack of confidence, Raj and Phoebe's over eagerness pushes them farther as outliers, while Amy and Ross just want to be loved.

CBS copied what worked on NBC's *Friends*. There is nothing wrong or illegal here—products and services are reverse engineered and recreated by competitors every day. Even a very basic competitive analysis would reveal what a targeted audience wants, and CBS saw a need for a *Friends*-type show again.

Friends was based in New York City, *TBBT* is based in California. Both areas are considered fringe by mainstream Americans. They're odd—New Yorkers crammed together on a little island and Californians waiting for the San Andreas to drop them into the sea. But that's part of the design; both locations are a part of the cast (similar to what Brian Eno said of recording studios being part of the band in Chapter 1).

Each deals with dating among the characters, weddings among the characters, pregnancies among the characters, and even pregnant weddings among the characters. Both shows cast Capuchin Monkeys in transitory roles, going so far as to connect the animals with the same character (Ross on *Friends* and Amy on *TBBT*). Each has a silly cat jingle (Smelly Cat on *Friends*, Soft Kitty on *TBBT*).

So, in reinventing this wheel, CBS wanted to recreate the sense that those kinds of friends are still around to watch on television. Rather than on the East coast, they'll be on the West. Different genders, different relationships, different careers, but still the adorable geeks America fell in love with 20 years ago.

My point in including this here is that *TBBT* and *Friends* are hardly unique. The history of entertainment is replete with other examples of movie and television executives using role equivalence over and over based on accepted templates:

A Man Wrongly Accused: An innocent man is incarcerated but escapes while being transferred due to the nefarious actions of others. He is pursued by a righteous cop who comes to recognize the mistreatment of justice that has occurred (Figure 10.3), *The Fugitive* and *Con Air*.

1993   1997

Figure 10.3 Men wrongly accused

Black and White "Buddy Films": A White guy on the edge with a dead wife (*Lethal Weapon*), a cheating wife (*Last Boy Scout*), or a lost wife (*Men in Black*), is saved by their fearless new Black partner (Figure 10.4).

Professional Woman and Annoying Sidekick: An uptight professional woman attains career success due to an unwanted, but loveably spirited

Figure 10.4 Black and White buddy films

male sidekick (Figure 10.5), *Remington Steele, Moonlighting, Castle,* and *Bones.*

Figure 10.5 Professional women and annoying sidekicks

This technique works cross-culturally as well. *One Day at a Time* was telecast on CBS from 1975 to 1984 featuring a divorced single mother raising two teenage daughters in Indianapolis. It was rewritten as a Cuban American military divorcee living with three generations in the same house.

Mad About You was an NBC sitcom that was telecast from 1992 to 1999. It too was repackaged and relocated, from New York City to Beijing, featuring young newlyweds finding their way through the first few years of marriage. The only real difference between the two is the switch from English to Mandarin. They even feature the same breed of dog—a Golden Retriever.

1975-1984

2016-2020

1992-1999

2016

Figure 10.6 Multicultural rewrites

Ok, I'm beating a dead horse here. But I'm trying to make a point— in evaluating start-up opportunities, investors are identical to television executives—they are afraid to fail. But unlike entertainment executives, these managers don't get nearly as many pitch sessions to evaluate and learn from, so they're going to take a bit longer to consider things.

Consciously or unconsciously they are evaluating a start-up opportunity in the context of a business model (and usually a market) they already understand. Perhaps more specifically, they are looking at the cast (the founders) and determining how similar they are (or aren't) to successful founders they've seen in the past. This will influence their decision in whether to support a new opportunity.

The overarching task is the same—funding. Television executives and start-up investors must put money upfront where it will be spent. It's not in some cushy escrow account. It is funding lights, camera, and action for the former, and programmers, engineers, and prototyping for the latter. Once spent, that money is gone, pure and simple, never to return.

So entrepreneurs should take a page from their Tinseltown colleagues and consider how to best position their concept in the light of what an investor wants to see. Here again, pointing out the advantage of corporate venture funding is useful.

If a corporation is actively looking for particular technologies, regional presence, or expansion into a new area, then start-ups should direct the pitch to that area as much as possible. If a start-up knows the corporation just withdrew from a technology that failed but it remains an area of interest, they may benefit from that timing.

But just like the big Hollywood studios, large corporations with good market intelligence are always monitoring their competition. If HUGE Corp invests in an artificial intelligence start-up, then GIANT Global is likely to follow soon. Allowing a competitor to get a one-up in a key technology area is foolish. Allowing them to create a technology portfolio—the start-up equivalent of NBC's "*Must See TV*" Thursday night lineup—is competitive suicide.

This also means copying is rampant. Stealing what works (or what you cannot buy), is a legitimate strategy. Look at the Snapchat/Instagram saga that's been going on for years. They're hardly alone. The same thing happened with voice commands (Siri/Alexa),[5] gesture controls (iOS/Android), and payment platforms (Stripe/Square).[6]

Steve Jobs supersized Pablo Picasso's mantra of "*good artists copy, great artists steal,*" bragging how Apple took many of their ideas from

Xerox PARC.[7] Real innovation is fleeting, and as soon as a clear market emerges for something it will be copied and improved upon. Better to do it yourself than be moved on by a competitor.

I'm not saying corporate executives will knee-jerk approve any start-up pitch they know is similarly being pursued by a competitor. Far from it. But if competitor movements, shareholder pressures, or annual reports clearly show an interest in a particular technology, it should give start-ups a hint of what corporations they should approach.

So as they say in Hollywood, get out there and *break a leg*!

CHAPTER 11

Start-Ups in the Supply Chain

In September 2019, Apple held its annual product release event at their Cupertino headquarters. CEO Tim Cook unveiled the new iPhone 11 Pro, which featured three rear-facing cameras utilizing "computational photography." This addition to Apple's signature device opened the technology into new areas including health care, autonomous vehicles, and more.

Computational photography is the use of mathematical software processing to produce images beyond the limitations of what a physical lens or sensor can capture on its own. The technology automates many of the functions needed to make the experience of point-and-shoot photography better.

Processing algorithms improve images by reducing motion blur and adding simulated depth of field. They can also improve color, contrast, and light range. While these enhancements are often featured on digital cameras, they are even more useful for smartphones and other applications where processor power can substitute for the array of optical lens choices that come with specialty DSLR cameras.

With computational photography, numerous images are taken at once from multiple angles and statistically cross-referenced. These images can be cut into tiles and blended, dropped to eliminate blur, or get the best detail from light/dark balance. As an example, the image stabilization of a DSLR camera's hardware lens is similarly achieved on a smartphone by using software to cross-reference data from its gyroscope.

Prior smartphone camera improvements have already impacted the consumer DSLR camera business, causing dramatic revenue drops in recent years. Industry leaders Nikon and Canon announced an additional 17 percent drop in sales during 1Q 2019.[1] Canon, seeing the consumer market slipping away, was changing its strategy. It told reporters it was *"taking measures to shift our business focus toward B2B, expanding our business sphere to automotive and industry use."*[2]

Apple historically prefers "getting it right vs getting it first," and the three-camera iPhone 11 Pro was no exception. Both Samsung and Huawei have already featured the technology in their higher priced phones.

Foxconn's Early Investment

In 2015, a Palo Alto-based start-up called Light.co was working on the idea of using math to overcome the physics limitations of optical lenses. Light.co's camera featured 16 individual lenses, creating a single photograph from up to 10 separate images that are digitally stitched together.[3] Light.co estimated that inserting their technology into a smartphone would add $60 to a maker's build of materials cost.[4]

Taiwan-based electronics giant Foxconn invested in Light.co at that time, which not only gave them the right to use the technology for their own purposes but it also allowed Foxconn to offer it to any of their other customers.[5] Foxconn, also known as Hon Hai Precision Industry Company, is a primary component supplier and contract manufacturer for Apple. It is Foxconn who does the lion's share of work in iPhone hardware and assembly.

Light.co spent two more years tweaking their software, but once they were able to demonstrate the capability, interest was high. In 2018, Light.co went on to raise an additional $100M from Softbank and the German camera brand Leica.[6] In February 2019, Light.co announced a joint development project with Sony to incorporate additional sensors to their system.[7]

Foxconn also invested early in a start-up called *SmartSense*, whose facial recognition system can identify an individual person in seconds from a file database of billions.[8] New surveillance cameras can identify people up to 45 kilometers away, applying Light Detection and Ranging, or LIDAR-like techniques to map reflected light.[9]

This technology has numerous other applications, from retail to health care. Banks use facial recognition to improve security and eliminate fraud,[10] and Duke University researchers were using earlier versions of the iPhone's rear-facing camera and algorithms to screen children for autism.[11] Analytics from multiple angles per-instance could advance these applications further. For Light.co and SmartSense, working with a large supply chain conglomerate like Foxconn opened many doors at once. Rather than pitching companies like Apple directly, it was able to attract a significant supply chain purveyor that opened doors across multiple industries.

Smile for the Camera

Retailers are using such facial recognition to estimate a customer's age, gender, or mood. Retail giant Proctor & Gamble previewed the Opte Precision Skincare handheld detector wand. Research fellow (and Opte inventor) Thomas Rabe told reporters "*I had to wait for cell phone cameras to become much better quality and micro-processing to go through 70,000 lines of code instantaneously.*"[12] When he began his research over a decade ago, the detector array was the size of a microwave oven.

The wand rolled out with a $599 price tag. Scanning at 200 frames per second as it rolls over a user's face, a thermal inkjet printer deposits microscopic drops of serum on skin spots to precisely match the skin around it. The user's movements provide the multiple viewing angles from a single camera lens. This results in the same goal as the iPhone 11 Pro's multiple lens array. Computational photography, capturing images from several angles, could bring similar applications to a much broader market, reducing costs.

This technology could also have an impact on digital therapeutics. Artificial intelligence (A/I) is making significant inroads for evaluating digital imagery files from CT, MRI, and X-ray machines. Rather than eliminating human jobs, A/I is helping humans do these jobs better. A/I can quickly sort through scans of healthy tissue, allowing physicians to focus their time and attention on scans that suggest the presence of disease.

Medical Imaging

GE Healthcare announced the Food and Drug Administration (FDA) had cleared their Critical Care Suite, the first approval of embedded A/I algorithms on a mobile X-ray device. The new application of A/I technology helped reduce cycle time from as long as 8 hours to under 15 minutes. Apple's new phone copies this model of placing the A/I algorithms on the device versus sending data up to a central cloud location for analysis. The President of GE Healthcare noted how *"X-Ray—the world's oldest form of medical imaging—just got a whole lot smarter, and soon, the rest of our offerings will too."*[13]

Computational photography for mental health applications on smartphones are another potential opportunity. Evaluating a consumer's probability for severe depression is one obvious application. Might such technology prevent suicides? Could it be applied to the recent rash of school shootings or public event mass attacks? The evidence suggests so.[14]

Telemedicine is another area that would seem ripe for such innovation. With the Covid-19 pandemic, the demand for telemedicine has skyrocketed.[15] Using stereo-camera smartphones, patients in remote areas can provide physicians at the top university research centers with imagery as good as if they were sitting across from them in the office. Telemedicine is increasingly popular—for patients, doctors, and health care programs—as the demand for medical professionals continues to outstrip supply.

Regardless of how computational photography is used in health care, it will create additional demand for storage solutions (cloud computing), cybersecurity assistance (HIIPA), file management (blockchain), and data science (analytics) that start-ups are in a unique position to fill.

Transportation

Autonomous vehicles are increasingly in the news as the big automakers partner with small technology start-ups. The big Silicon Valley players, who've never been popular among the Detroit crowd, are increasingly on the periphery. Although Waymo has Renault and Nissan as customers, Uber has Volvo, and GM Cruise has Honda, these are not groundbreaking innovators in transportation or in autonomous technology. Smaller players have raced in to fill the needs of the big automotive brands.

Aurora has the widest aperture of clients, though Hyundai was evidently unhappy about sharing, and entered into a $4B joint venture with

Aptiv a couple of years ago.[16] Ford is sharing its previous Argo investment with VW, concentrating on autonomous systems, while its new German partner focuses on electric vehicles (EVs). Apple meanwhile picked up the assets of Drive.AI in a fire sale when the autonomous software start-up prepared to shut down (Figure 11.1).[17]

Figure 11.1 *Autonomous vehicle start-ups and their benefactors*

One name is notably absent from this mix—*Tesla*. Among his eccentricities, Elon Musk has a strong antipathy for LIDAR technology.[18] "LIght Detection And Ranging" measures distance to a target by illuminating it with a laser and analyzing the reflected light with a sensor. LIDAR is a significant aspect of most major autonomous vehicle platforms, as well as a substantial cost.

Aurora considers LIDAR so important it acquired Blackmore,[19] and Argo did the same with Princeton Lightwave.[20] Drive.AI also incorporates LIDAR into its system, using technology from the Massachusetts Institute of Technology (MIT) to try to automate the process.[21] The expense and difficulty in developing LIDAR technology was at the heart of the trade secrets lawsuit Google filed against former employee Anthony Levandowski when he allegedly took 14,000 confidential files with him to a new job at Uber.[22]

Yet Musk, with the credibility of over 500,000 Teslas on the roads,[23] mocks the technology mercilessly. He may have a point. Researchers at Cornell University have used simple stereo cameras mounted in a windshield to provide the same function as expensive LIDAR arrays. Placing the cameras higher, what they call a more "birds-eye view," radically increases the accuracy over the more traditionally mounted "front-view" camera position.

Here again, computational photography could make a significant impact. Like the Opte pen moving across skin, a vehicle's movement provides multiple viewpoints of the same object. By mathematically scoring those views with knowledge of the vehicle's speed and direction, computational photography has the potential to provide a unique alternative to LIDAR and other expensive technologies.

Recall the failure of Siemen's autonomous-rigged classic Mustang at the Goodwood Auto show in 2018.[24] Forgoing sensor gear, the vehicle's technology centered around highly detailed maps, yet still failed to navigate the course. There simply is no substitute for *localized* and *speedy* data inputs for autonomous vehicle systems. Downtown Boston blanketed in February snow would be a similarly formidable obstacle for LIDAR and Radar-equipped cars, but computational photography has the potential to not just overcome this but also to leverage it to prove its efficacy against these more expensive alternatives.

TuSimple, backed by Nvidia and Sina (China's Weibo owners) is an autonomous semitruck start-up. Like many such firms it is seeking a "full stack solution," but it has taken the unusual position of being camera-centric. TuSimple believes that LIDAR accuracy fails at distances greater than 150 meters when traveling at higher speeds, (as highway trucks do). The firm claims their camera-based system has a range of 1,000 meters, and tested its accuracy via 3 to 5 trips per day on Arizona highways.[25]

Autonomous technology has other applications, including for drones. Cameras are ubiquitous on aerial and terrestrial drones, so the ability to avoid saddling them with expensive and heavy sensor arrays meets a customer need. Researchers at the University of Zurich recently used "event cameras," systems that only send data when the view within its field of vision changes.[26] Reducing the frame refresh reduced the data demand, improving response times. Researchers demonstrated the technique by throwing a ball at a quadcopter, which was able to easily navigate away from it while still holding its position.

Adjacent Fields

Foxconn is one of many contract manufacturers who can leverage start-up investments in one area across multiple customers, markets, and industries. Owing to their sheer size, and their history of innovation in assembling iPhones for Apple, they are often viewed as thought leaders in this area.

Their camera technology has application across many customers, from augmented reality (A/R) glasses to automobiles. In 2020, the Cult of Mac website reported Foxconn was working on MicroLED lenses for augmented reality headsets targeting industrial and medical device markets.[27] This follows on Foxconn's investment in a MicroLED start-up called Lux in 2017.[28] Foxconn will reportedly also be the manufacturer for Apple's future A/R glasses.[29]

Apple tends to be very coy when talking publicly about A/R. But support for STARBOARD, Apple's stereoscopic A/R headset project, was included in their iOS 13 update.[30] So it at least appears Apple has plans for such multiple lens camera arrays. Given the shutdown of A/R start-ups including Daqri,[31] ODG,[32] and Meta,[33] Apple is likely taking their time to ensure the price point meets the market requirements.

Foxconn knows how to apply technological advantage across its vast manufacturing base, to include its interests in automobiles. They are a contract manufacturer for the EV start-up Fisker.[34] Foxconn recently purchased the Ohio manufacturing site of Lordstown Motors, which they will operate to assemble Lordstown's Endurance pickup truck. The same site will also reportedly be where Foxconn builds Fisker's EVs as well.[35] Lordstown, with a federal investigation underway and several top executives resigning, needed a cash infusion and substantial manufacturing help to remain afloat.[36]

As I've written previously, start-up failure is not the same as personal failure. Some start-ups are simply too early, either with their innovation or their market acceptance. Supply chain giants like Foxconn can leverage their investment in and partnerships with innovative start-ups to bridge the gap between advanced technologies and commercialization.

CHAPTER 12

Electric Vehicles

The electric vehicle (EV) market has matured quite suddenly. Springing out from behind the hype around autonomous vehicles, electrics have leapfrogged in every measure from technology to politics. While consumer attention has been focused on a single brand—Tesla—numerous young start-ups are poised to further the technology faster than industry leaders had predicted.

This creates a chaotic market for industry leaders such as General Motors (GM), Ford, and other Detroit stalwarts. And if we look back a bit at recent history, the Tesla story takes on an interesting new dimension.

In the documentary "*Who Killed the Electric Car*," filmmaker Chris Paine outlines in detail the lengths major automobile manufacturers, particularly GM engaged in to suppress electric vehicles (EVs). In 1990, the California Air Resources Board passed the Zero Emissions Vehicles mandate, which required domestic automobile manufacturers to start offering EVs to continue selling gasoline-powered cars in the state of California.

GM offered their first originally designed electric car, the "EV1," from 1996 to 1999. But they would not sell the cars outright, instead only offering them through a lease program to customers primarily in California. As the documentary shows, at the end of the lease period, GM refused to let customers purchase the cars. Instead, it collected them all, then summarily crushed and buried the entire series. Other than a couple of lucky units that were whisked away into museums or private collections, it is as if the EV1 never existed.

A year after the great 2008 financial bailout of the automobile industry by the federal government, Chief Executive Officer Rick Wagoner was forced out of GM. He later called his killing of the EV1 his "*greatest mistake as a CEO*."[1] It is ironic then that he subsequently came to embrace EVs by joining the Board of Directors for ChargePoint, which operates a network of EV charging stations.[2]

The dearth of recharging options for long-distance driving has slowed consumer acceptance of EVs. Commercial acceptance however appears to be moving forward rather aggressively—not simply in local delivery vehicles, but also in aviation, marine applications, and drone services of every stripe. Indeed, commercial applications are developing across multiple areas—batteries, data science, cybersecurity, inventory management, and supply chain. Start-up companies are quickly filling this vacuum for the unique needs of commercial and industrial operators.

There are several start-up incubators dedicated to EVs. These include government initiatives such as the Nevada Electric Vehicle Incubator, the Rochester Electric Vehicle Incubator, and Los Angeles Cleantech Incubator for Zero Emission Vehicles. There are nonprofit efforts including the Huddle coworking accelerator for EV start-ups[3] and Europe's IMPACT connected car incubator.[4] There are also commercial entities operated by automotive brands including Jaguar/Land Rover[5] and VW Group.[6]

But none of these endeavors address commercial EVs and the specific needs of business model problems, opportunities, and disruptions. Most of the organizations above are focused solely on the automotive market—none are addressing aviation, boats and ships, drone applications, or scooters and cycles. Similarly, none are focused on the industrial markets of EV technology such as forklifts or warehouse robotics.

Start-ups rushing in to fill this void have an advantage over incumbent players. While Detroit automakers are experts on vehicle hardware engineering, they have zero experience in attracting specialists in data analytics, cybersecurity, (battery) chemical technology, and (connected) communications systems. With commercial fleet vehicles moving to the forefront of the industry, start-ups focusing on warehousing, trucking, logistics, and supply chain will see huge opportunities.

Though autonomous vehicles will have a slow but steady impact on the transportation industry, EVs are creating a significant impact in a much shorter timeframe. Part of this is because the concerns consumers have over electric platforms are very different from those of commercial fleet operators.

Switching over to EVs is no simple undertaking. It requires a fundamental upgrade to everything from vehicle bays to maintenance to capital allocation. Then add in the changes that occur as commercial vehicles become true "mobile" devices—interacting with city grids, cellular networks, satellites, and smart phone applications.

How will businesses manage this? How will they handle the torrent of data, most of which they've never dealt with before? Who owns this information? Who is allowed to access, analyze, or act on it? How will small and medium sized businesses secure their data from hackers, and how will managers prevent ransomware from accessing corporate networks?

In 2021, Ford announced it was introducing an all-electric F-150 pickup truck. Fully 8 percent of the U.S. workforce currently uses an F-series truck in their day-to-day job,[7] and CEO Jim Farley told investors in February 2021 that mid-sized companies were *running their businesses on Post It Notes. They're very underserved.*[8] The big game changer here is how start-ups can effectively compete against legacy manufacturers.

This disruption begins at the factory where the cars are made. Internal combustion engines can have over two thousand moving parts—EV motors can have as few as twenty![9] That means massive change as assembly plants will need fewer employees (already causing GM contract negotiations problems), less warehousing (and fewer warehouse employees), a smaller supply chain, less regulatory problems (fewer petroleum products to store in bulk), and a more modular assembly design that is essentially plug and play.

From an operational standpoint, consumers are irrationally afraid their car's batteries are going to die. There are 100,000 more gas stations than there are charging stations in the United States, but despite 98 percent of all consumer trips being local and short duration, they're still afraid. (That's what makes it irrational!) Twenty percent of EV owners in California gave up and returned to internal combustion engines.[10] Not because they'd had a recharging problem; they just feared having one!

But none of these perceived problems are relevant for commercial vehicles, quite the contrary in fact. They see great advantages with EVs. First, emissions regulations are getting tighter. (Watch California and weep—it will move across the country.) Second, overall costs of oil-based energy are rising quickly, but electricity's is not. Finally, charging infrastructure is getting built, and for local commercial operations, it's quite simple.

Commercial vehicle operators benefit from a *"Boomerang Effect."* They begin and end from the same place over the course of a shift, be it a delivery vehicle or a service truck. I'm talking about small vehicles here, typically Class 3 to 5 trucks making local runs and returning to the same place every night where they can be recharged. The stop-and-go nature of these routes means regenerative brakes will keep batteries charged longer than one-way highway runs, extending their range.

What's more, energy and transportation are the two biggest greenhouse gas emitters in the United States. This will provide start-up firms with potential funding sources dedicated the environment, cleanup, and transportation upgrades (Figure 12.1).

Greenhouse gas emissions by industry sector

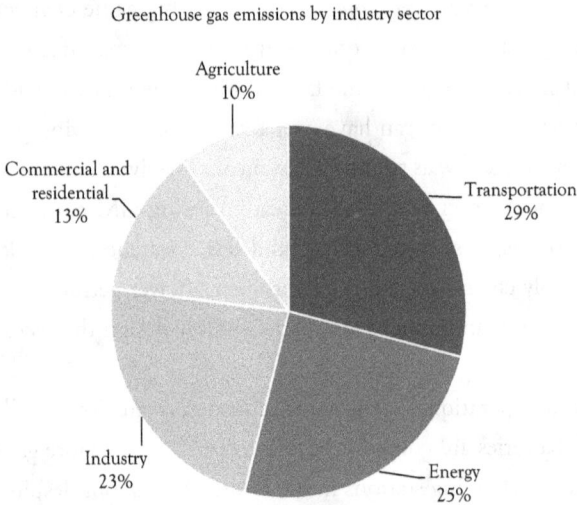

Figure 12.1 EPA greenhouse gas emissions by sector

Source: EPA, 2019.

But this potential is not restricted to delivery vans and trucks. Through grants, consulting services, and contracted research start-ups will address EV platforms beyond the automobile into autonomous drones, warehouse robotics, aircraft, and boating. These opportunities are not only for the vehicles themselves, but also for:

- Preparing local and regional power grids for the coming load increases

- Recycling batteries as uninterrupted power supplies for schools, hospitals, and more
- Academic/corporate partnerships to retain and retrain the current labor force
- Fostering EV acceptance by supplying courtesy vehicles to hotels and Airbnbs

These changes have started, but there are many more just over the horizon that incumbent players are only beginning to wrestle with. Continental wrote off billions as parts demand shifts from gas engines to electric.[11] Their competitor Lear has a new CFO retooling their business for an electric future.[12] Marinas will lose not just fuel sales, but also mechanics services, spare parts, maintenance, and more. How will they make up for these revenue losses? Air cargo start-ups are booming due to e-commerce, mainly because 30 percent of passenger aircraft had shut down due to Covid.[13] How can they adjust to electric jet engines?

The impact of EVs is being felt across the employment spectrum, from GM's cantankerous contract negotiations[14] to a high school auto shop program shifting from crankcases to electric conversions.[15]

It is difficult to overstate the impact EVs will have. Daimler announced massive layoffs due to sagging demand for gas-powered vehicles[16] while concurrently introducing a new electric garbage truck for municipalities.[17] GM reversed a planned closure for its last remaining Detroit manufacturing site. Now it is assembling electric shuttle buses as a contract manufacturer for a start-up, hoping to build their own electric pickup trucks there in the future.[18]

Competition in the U.S. pickup truck market is fierce, so the changes coming to commercial use vehicles will be formidable. Ford is busy redesigning its heavy-duty F-150 into miniature offices, complete with desks and wide bandwidth WIFI.[19] Meanwhile, the iconic delivery vehicle designs of UPS, FedEx, and Amazon Prime are being reimagined for an electric-only future.[20] Fleet operators like Coca Cola are beta testing EVs for delivery, forklift, and even airport ground services.

While the technological pieces of these innovations are goldmines for start-ups, they are terrifying for established enterprises. The typical automobile dealer will suffer a 35 percent decline in maintenance revenues from the loss of two of their top three shop revenues—oil changes and brake service—with the transition to EVs.[21] *Perhaps they can make up this revenue loss in working with local start-ups!*

As if to underscore this near-term uncertainty, researchers recently hacked into automobile charging stations, disclosing just how vulnerable they are to ransomware and other cyber intrusions.[22] Such disruption isn't just on the ground either—the first commercial electric airplane began test flights in 2019.[23]

Rolls Royce recently announced their electric airplane was the fastest in the world (Figure 12.2).[24] Crowned as the *"Spirit of Innovation,"* its 400-kW electric motor delivered the equivalent of 535 horsepower, reaching a top speed of 387 mph during test flights, breaking the prior record set by Siemens in 2017. Part of the project's funding came from the British government and the Aerospace Technology Institute.[25] A typical battery-science partner for a firm like Rolls Royce? Not at all, which no doubt contributed significantly to its success!

Figure 12.2 Rolls Royce's spirit of innovation electric plane

This type of disruption is not for the faint of heart; even a corporation built on innovation can find the EV market difficult to navigate. After several years of expensive efforts, design and engineering pioneer Dyson decided to close its EV division. Billionaire founder and Chairman James Dyson had predicted his firm's *fantastic car* would be on roads by 2020. But in the end, the business challenges (not the technical ones), proved too overwhelming.[26] Here again, start-ups without these legacy overhead costs are better able to pivot to new business models.

So how do companies with a large vehicle fleet prepare for the disruption this technology will bring? How do they predict business costs, revenues, and profit margins as they transition to a battery-centric future? The personnel, political, and performance minefields that must be navigated are considerable. Commercial/industrial companies, whether market leaders or luddites being dragged into the new century, need help figuring this future out. Partnering with start-up companies will be the saving grace for many.

How will these systems effect urban planning? Or public transportation infrastructure? How will it change delivery services, home health monitoring, and child care options? Jobs will certainly change as a result, but how will hiring change to accommodate it? What will this mean for work from home versus working in an office? What impact does this have on the commercial and industrial real estate markets? These, and a host of other questions, are ripe with opportunities for innovative start-ups looking to make their mark.

Perhaps nowhere is the impact of EVs more evident than in the state of Tennessee. GM is building EVs in Spring Hill, and Nissan is building them in Smyrna. Between the two the Volunteer State is already the number three producer of EVs in the nation[27]—and this is before Volkswagen's new EV plant in Chattanooga begins production in 2022 (Figure 12.3).[28] Not to be left out, Ford announced in September it was building a $5B EV plant in West Tennessee, the largest single investment in the state's history.[29]

Figure 12.3 VW's electric vehicle plant in Chattanooga, TN

Start-ups will find a ready market as these firms will need agile suppliers, vendors, and service providers to make their ambitious production numbers work. Fortunately for entrepreneurs, Tennessee is a very start-up-friendly state.

The Tennessee Valley Authority (TVA), a federally owned electric utility, is the largest public power company in the United States. When it announced it was converting at least half of their light and medium duty trucks to electric power by 2030, people noticed.[30] Leading by example, 1,200 vehicles will make the transition from gas to rechargeable batteries over the next decade.

We can expect other large fleet owners to follow TVA's lead, particularly with public–private partnerships like Drive Electric Tennessee deconflicting the efforts of state agencies, auto manufacturers, and universities.[31] This coordinated effort has grabbed global attention, with battery makers LG Chem, SK Innovation, and Novonix opening or planning new regional facilities to support the industry.

Start-ups can fulfill several product and service needs in the EV ecosystem. Through a combination of available capital, fast response times, and lower overhead costs they can leverage people and innovations where new demand awaits.

CHAPTER 13

Start-Ups at War

The first start-up I ever worked in was called Spatial Data Analytics, or SPADAC. It was started by two guys who worked for the National Reconnaissance Office (NRO). The NRO owned a software package for analyzing satellite imagery that was extremely complex and very difficult to operate, much less use efficiently.

The two founders thought there was some potential though—they thought they could do some very cool stuff in the commercial sector with the system. So they pitched the NRO on taking the software out to the "real" world. To their credit, the NRO agreed, on one condition.

They would have to grant the federal government an unrestricted license to whatever improvements they made to the system. Any upgrades to the application or the underlying code had to be shared free and clear in perpetuity. They readily agreed.

SPADAC went on to get contracts from Google Earth and the Department of Defense. I was hired to work on a team delivering analytic support and services to U.S. Special Operations Command (SOCOM).

SOCOM manages the Special Operations fighters of the U.S. military all over the world—Navy SEALS, Army Rangers, Air Force Pararescue Jumpers (PJs), and more. From a single building on MacDill Air Force Base in Tampa, Florida, a casual observer can see how discrete U.S. military power is applied around the world.

Most of this work remains classified, which made pitching new customers rather difficult. When all your examples consist of military campaigns that rely on secrecy to be successful, we struggled with ways to describe what we do and how we do it to ordinary commercial customers. Fortunately, my children came to the rescue.

My son and daughter were young and attended middle school together. While my wife and I saw the precursors of adolescence rearing its ugly head on occasion, puberty had not quite yet arrived. They were, alas, still children.

I couldn't help but notice something when I dropped them off one day, and oddly enough, it turned into a great example of how to explain time and space analytics to everyone.

Some of the boys were playing football in the parking lot—someone found a ball and an impromptu pick-up game was underway. Sitting in my car I had a clear, unobstructed view of the game and the players. But a thought soon struck me—what if I *couldn't* see them? What if I could only see the abstract movements of nondescript individuals on a remote screen? What could I determine about what was going on?

From the vantage point of my car, I could see everything clearly. The boys were playing ball to show off in front of the girls, though they don't yet understand why. The girls were pretending to not watch the boys, though they don't really know why yet either. But even if I couldn't see them, I could empirically analyze all their movements and identify, (based on probabilities), the boys from the girls from their movements in time and space. Statistically speaking, boys play football, most girls don't.

So let's assume for a moment that I couldn't see anything at all—that I could only see unattributed movements provided by sensor telemetry displayed on a computer screen. This could be anything—infrared strobes, radio tags, or similar "stand-off" technology of each player in and around the parking lot. What could I determine about the events taking place?

I would know it's a football game because I can ascertain the basic outline of the "field" being used over and over by both "teams." (This would provide me a statistical probability of football over soccer or even rugby, based on the player's movements.) I could even recognize the patterns of specific football plays. Though I would not see the ball from any remote location, I could estimate its position from each play to the next, based on the movements of the players on the (parking lot) field.

From this data I could determine the extroverts (playing the game) versus introverts (watching it). Based on player positions, I could identify the quarterback—he is likely the leader. The wide receiver is likely the fastest boy on the field. The blockers, on both sides, are likely the biggest, strongest, and most aggressive boys on the field.

I can determine who the emerging leaders are among this group of otherwise disparate boys. Who is consistently in the "most important" roles? Do these positions rotate among the players, or do only select individuals take them? Repeated behavior, correlational statistics, and probability metrics will identify the emergent leaders even if we don't know their names or what they look like. All I need to "see" is their behaviors.

What SPADAC called spatial analytics is more broadly recognized in the commercial world as behavioral economics, analyzing people's behavior based solely on what they do. It is a powerful new field of science that is expanding rapidly.

So what good is it? Behavioral economics is analyzing cyberattacks based on learned metrics from prior hacks.[1] Cybersecurity firm DarkTrace had a client who was attacked through a rudimentary machine learning tool that observed and monitored "normal" network user behavior. It then used that analysis to mimic the normal behavior and blend in with expected traffic, making it harder to detect.

Military planners analyze the fighting campaigns of allies and foes alike. How do they move thousands of personnel, tons of equipment, as well as food and fuel to sustain a forward presence, when they are thousands of miles away from home? The details of these activities—how and why foreign decision makers make the choices they do—has long been a target of intelligence collection.

The same is happening in the commercial world. Microsoft has sold over 30 million Xbox systems; Sony has sold over 50 million Play Station units.[2] Competition among developers to hook gamers into long-term play is fierce, as the video game industry is now a $100B business worldwide.[3]

Knowing when a player might get bored—and log out of the game—is critical. Knowing what inducements will keep gamers playing, slicing and dicing data across age, gender, ethnicity, location, and socioeconomic dimensions, is worth millions of revenue dollars.[4] While many of us grew up on arcade games and Atari cartridge systems, the Internet has now globalized the industry.

Video game makers are increasingly finding that the behavioral data of their users is a common "insider threat" by employees and contractors who will sell this information to competing developers. In 2015, the Federal Bureau of Investigation arrested a former employee of Game-Zone as he was boarding a flight to China.[5] Among his carry-on items was downloaded data from his former employer on millions of "*Game of War: Fire Age*" users broken down by time, location, age, and other dimensions.[6]

Game makers see a significant amount of revenue from these "add on" sales; the option to purchase additional "lives," tools, and other services *inside* the game.[7] A popular gaming keyboard was discovered to have a built-in keystroke logger that sent all behavioral typing data to a server owned by Alibaba Group, the China-based tech giant.[8]

Polish video game developer CD Projekt Red was the target of a ransomware attack a couple of years ago with hackers claiming to have internal data about the upcoming release of their game *Cyberpunk 2077*.[9] So why is such behavioral analysis important? Because it literally can change the world!

When I was working at SPADAC, one of the supervisors brought me an evaluation a young analyst had done that he wanted my opinion on. This was a budding software engineer, and he was using his developer account with Twitter to play around with an idea.

One of the advantages to having a developer account was that Twitter provides real-time data to work with as engineers develop plug-ins to make the platform better. This young man asked for such access, requesting Twitter data for early 2011 in Cairo, Egypt. He showed me what the Twitter feeds looked like when a mobile device's GPS data was plotted out on a standard military map grid.

I stared at a map of Cairo with hundreds of superimposed dots that coalesced over time into three "hotspots" of activity. I had no idea what I was looking at and admitted as much. "*They are finding each other*," the young analyst impatiently explained.

The Twitter feeds showed movement from (stationary) desktop PCs to smartphones, and as they did so, the Tweeters were locating each other on the streets of Cairo. Applying a rudimentary social network analysis, he discovered that as they found each other in the Twittersphere they subsequently also found each other physically.

The average distance among these Tweeting protestors shrank over a short period of time, from an average of 65 meters to less than 12.

"I wasn't aware you could read Arabic," I said.

"I can't," the young man replied.

He hadn't read a single Tweet in his analysis and to this day neither have I. Yet he was able to conduct what was, to the best of my knowledge, the most profound analysis of the Arab Spring ever produced. Activists were finding each other in real time, and by culling through the behavioral data, he could identify by phone number, (and therefore by name), the 10 people *most* responsible for the fall of Egyptian President Hosni Mubarak.

From the other side of the world, with just his laptop and freely available commercial sources, a young start-up idealist identified the handful of people that Mubarak could have quietly taken out and nobody would have known a thing. He could have remained in power.

Alternatively, the opposition could have determined the *exact* people to supply money, guns (which were ultimately unnecessary), or more smartphones and hastened Mubarak's fall a lot faster. As uprisings spread to other parts of the Middle East that summer, it was not hard to imagine the implications of this.

It's not scary that this young man pulled this analysis off. What is scary is that any banana republic, nonstate actor, or criminal element can do it as well. There are uprisings taking place all over Iran; don't think for a moment the mullahs aren't considering what happened in Cairo. As the technology for remote monitoring gets more commonplace, the analysis for using that data gets more predictive and accurate every day.

Amazon has long used individual buying patterns to identify things we may be interested in. Target infamously sent a teenager coupons for diapers and baby wipes when they determined she was pregnant, even before her own father knew.[10] Instagram photos can reveal indicators of depression.[11] Facebook allows advertisers to textually analyze posts to slot paid advertisers to promising members.[12] None of this is theoretical. It is happening now. And military strategists should consider how our adversaries will apply these techniques to their own purposes.

Back in 2017, Russian agents were suspected of poaching user data from the smartphones of North Atlantic Treaty Organizations, or NATO soldiers in theater, including Americans.[13] Postings through social media apps provide the names of soldier's families, and the GPS chip provides

the soldier's exact location. Unknown agents have walked up to our ser-
vicemen out on a weekend pass and commented about their family members back home by name—a harassment technique that's no doubt doing
wonders for morale and scaring security leaders across the continent.

Since the 9/11 attacks two decades ago, the federal government has
learned the value of start-up innovations. Osama Bin Laden, the architect
of the World Trade Center attacks was famously killed in 2011 by a Navy
SEAL Team incursion into Pakistan. But how did the SEALS know he
was there? A start-up company providing discrete data mining services
allegedly played a significant role.

Palantir Technologies helps big companies like United Airlines optimize its routing systems as well as Merck with drug discovery.[14] But it also
helped the Justice Department investigate Bernie Madoff's complicated
Ponzi scheme[15] and, according to many, helped the Defense Department
track down Bin Laden. But Palantir is hardly alone.

While prime contractors such as Lockheed and General Dynamics
hold multiyear, multibillion dollar federal contracts, they subsequently
subcontract a lot of the specialized operational activities contained
in those contracts to start-up companies like SPADAC and Palantir.
But why?

Because start-ups like these, created by innovative founders, identify
a need and develop the means to fulfill it. Sometimes their customers
are corporations and sometimes they are government agencies. Increasingly, they are both. The big companies keep their government clients
happy, and the start-ups get long-term contracts by partnering with an
established player. Like Foxconn's investments and partnerships with
start-ups to better serve Apple, it's a win–win.

Abu Bakr al-Baghdadi was the terrorist leader of the Islamic State of
Iraq, (ISIS). In addition to killing many innocent Iraqi Muslims across
his so-called Caliphate, al-Baghdadi also brutally raped and killed an
American aid worker named Kayla Mueller.[16] As a result, American
military personnel were especially keen on tracking him down.

ISIS was one of the most financially successful terrorist groups in
history. A CNN/Money analysis of their far-flung operations showed
how the group distanced itself from Al Qaeda's model of relying on
wealthy donors to finance operations.[17] In one bold move, ISIS seized

over $400M from Mosul's Central Bank in 2014.[18] Young companies like New York-based Flashpoint provide specialized services in analyzing illicit financial transactions among terrorist groups, including ISIS.[19]

U.S. Special Operations forces chased al-Baghdadi into a tunnel under his safe house. Rather than be captured alive he detonated the suicide vest he was wearing, killing himself and three of his children.[20] The raid into Syria to capture him was codenamed "Operation Kayla Mueller," which her parents called "*an amazing gift.*"[21]

Small companies have an outsized impact when their innovations lead to game-changing actions like the elimination of a global terrorists like Bin Laden or al-Baghdadi. Unfortunately, there will likely be a need for more of this in the future rather than less.

CHAPTER 14

3D Print Start-Ups

There is a famous story of IBM executives visiting a young *wunderkind* named Bill Gates back in 1980. Planning their new PC computer, IBM wanted his start-up—Microsoft—to provide their operating system.[1] The contract was straightforward; Gates charged IBM a flat fee of $200K for development and up to $500K for any additional engineering work. He gave IBM the rights to DOS and other programs it could bundle into their new PC. But he also stipulated IBM could use the operating system for no additional fees or pay royalty payments if Microsoft alone could license the software to other firms.

IBM was planning products—Microsoft was planning a platform.

In turning a single operating system into an ecosystem for launching many other computer brands, Microsoft created an innovation platform that allowed other firms to create follow-on products and services. A cheap global operating system license allowed the production of low-cost hardware by firms around the world.

In a broad stroke, platforms connect people—either as individuals, employees, or groups organized around a common interest. But they are people-centric even though they incorporate computers, smartphones, and other linked devices. Platforms become business models when they network communities across multiple dimensions.

There are platforms for connecting work associates (LinkedIn), buyers and sellers (Amazon), or family and friends (Facebook). Perhaps it is no surprise then that Microsoft was an early investor in Facebook, no doubt recognizing a kindred spirit looking for an opportunity.[2] It is a model that has many implications for Additive Manufacturing, *aka* 3D Printing.

It would not be too far off the mark to characterize 3D printing as the manufacturing industry's *Boulevard of Broken Dreams*. Early on, the technology was described as a game changer for making products and government agencies devoted considerable resources to it. With price as no object, these early innovators weren't constrained by what was a good business—they instead focused on pushing the art of the possible. And some of their developments are indeed amazing.

The Oak Ridge National Laboratory (ORNL) outside of Knoxville, Tennessee, was an early experimenter in additive technologies, with a budget and thought leadership that allowed them to be creative despite the significant hardware and raw material costs.

ORNL 3D printed a Shelby Cobra convertible—not simply pieces, but the entire vehicle (other than tires, glass, and electronics). The car has now become ORNL's most popular "eye candy." This is no static mockup—Energy Secretaries Ernest Moniz, Rick Perry, and Thomas Zacharia have each driven it around the Lab's parking lot.[3] But it's hardly their only achievement. ORNL also 3D printed a miniature submarine for Navy SEAL Teams to further demonstrate the potential for on-demand vehicle production (Figure 14.1).[4]

Figure 14.1 3D printed car and submersible from Oak Ridge National Labs

While these unique one-off products are impressive (and driving the Cobra is a cool perk for every Energy Secretary), they have the additional benefit of moving public perception. When national laboratories demonstrate the art of the possible, the science of the possible soon follows. Once that science is understood, the business of commercializing begins, and Additive Manufacturing is no different.

A couple of companies have come and gone including MatterFab[5] and Electroloom,[6] while a few larger firms such as Carbon, Stratasys, and Desktop Metal have grown, albeit in fits and starts. From raw materials in polymers, to resins, to carbon fiber, and several types of metal, the technology is developing into multiple industries from medical devices to aviation to automotive components. While building 3D printers is relatively straightforward, operating them—as a business of *selling* the 3D printed items—can be very difficult.

As Bill Gates did with Microsoft, the successful operators appear to be successful not because of their printer hardware or even because of their raw materials. They've created unique platforms for providing their services. They appear to differentiate along three different models based on Personalization, Performance, or Preference:

- **Personalize Model**—customized for each customer, so the necessary cost premium is justified.
- **Performance Model**—supply chain performance by decreasing shipping time, with speed overcoming the cost barrier.
- **Preference Model**—a service bureau offering low-frequency parts (distinct niche markets) on a build-on-demand basis, essentially mass prototyping.

What is key is understanding the mix of structural dynamics within the platforms for these three models. For the personalization model there is a very high design mix for each customer. Those customers are low in number, and the volume count is even lower, including one time only. Any "repeat" business means starting from scratch with a new design.

The Performance model has a low design mix—most of the designs are fixed, even "building" (printing) on the customer's site, eliminating shipping costs entirely. If the costs can be spread across multiple customers in near proximity, there's a real chance to make this work, but again, the volume count is extremely low.

Finally, the Preference model, where design is cosmetic versus custom and the customer count is very low, but the aggregated niche volumes can be quite high. The scaled personalization is cosmetic versus structural, allowing for mass customization that, added together, reflect the more typical economies of scale.

Rather than detail three successes or three failures, I'd like to instead outline three platform examples—one very successful, one taking a deliberate pause, and the third an unfortunate (but likely only temporary) disappointment (Figure 14.2).

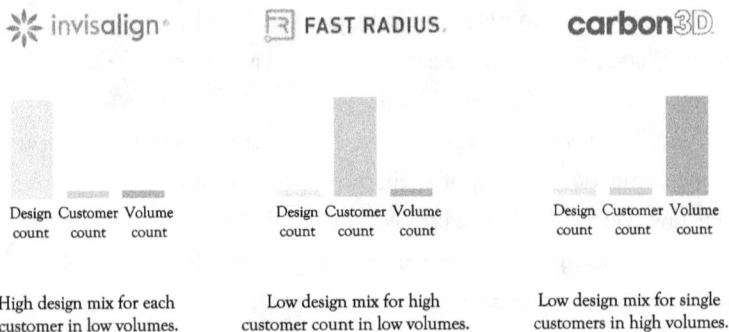

Figure 14.2 Business strategies in 3D printing

Personal Model

Few start-ups have mastered this platform approach quite as well as Invisalign Technologies. After breaking into the orthodontics world 20 years ago with a radical concept for replacing braces to correct teeth, they've become a dental unicorn and forever changed oral health care.

A scanning wand captures thousands of digital images a second in the patient's mouth. These photos are compiled to create a three-dimensional model. A predictive software application then maps a proposed sequential movement of the teeth over time. The models are used to 3D-print personalized casts of the patient's teeth that are the die molds to make the aligners that move the teeth around.

Invisalign supplies the scanning software, the predictive modeling, renderings of what the in-process dispositions will be like, and even how the patient's future smile will appear. Dentists can adjust the process in real time, showing patients where they are in treatment, adjusting along the way as necessary.

The casting of molds was previously a time-intensive endeavor that orthodontists did themselves. Mold resolution was critical to patient care; the more detail that was evident, the better the treatment would be. But patients were nervous about molds—the weird-looking dental cups and blue goop appeared like something from a B-rated horror movie. Adults were afraid they would choke and children frequently threw up, so it was a task ripe for start-up disruption!

When Invisalign first emerged it was pricey. Dental professionals were required to take classes to learn a proprietary software platform, a case management system that created visualizations for both the dentist and patient. The Invisalign scanning tool was $20K out of a dentist's pocket, but the technology was so good, and patients were so happy to have an alternative, the classic cup-and-goop method is rarely used anymore.

Dentists were invited to Costa Rica to see the production facility firsthand. But the selling point was clear; more patients could be pushed through the office via Invisalign than with traditional metal braces. Yes it might cost more, but the process was better for dental pros and patients alike.

A 45-minute braces appointment could be reduced to under 20 minutes with Invisalign. Dental practices didn't need to worry with bands, brackets, or wires. The shorter appointments allowed staff to interact more with patients, review their progress together, move to the next aligner in the series, and shoo the patient out before scheduling a return in 4 to 6 weeks.

What was important early on was identifying which procedures Invisalign could do and which it couldn't. As the company evolved, it has been able to perform more complicated procedures. The sophistication of the software allowed dentists to do more without requiring the same "chair time" as other options. These time costs were transferred from the examination chair and moved to the patient's leisure time at home.

Rather than dealing with unscheduled appointments for broken bracket hardware, dentists could simply order a replacement plastic aligner over the phone. No office visit was needed to get a patient back on track. Personnel management was streamlined, inventory was reduced, and more patients could be seen in each week—a very compelling business case.

Invisalign is now recycling the 3D molds used to make their aligners, nearing a point where they can 3D-print the aligners directly, without using a mold at all. Given the improvements to stereolithographic (SLA) printing techniques and harder plastics, this will simplify the process even more when it is complete.

Performance Model

Beginning in 2014, UPS saw a trajectory shift from conventional to digital processes. They viewed digital as the 4th modality after ground, ocean, and air transportation. Additive manufacturing was a means for efficiently making smaller quantities of items. Less storage, less shipping, and operational cost savings were among the obvious benefits.

According to CapGemini, the last mile of delivery can produce up to 41 percent of logistics costs.[7] This is Supply Chain 101, something UPS knows exceptionally well. (I worked for UPS in my undergraduate days, loading boxes onto delivery trucks early in the morning before heading to class.) But taking raw material at one site, then manufacturing and delivering a finished part to customers at a second (or even third) site is a wholly different business model.

Realizing they shouldn't simply dismiss the trend UPS sought a way to leverage their 1000+ warehouse locations worldwide. Their strategy was (and likely remains) to build 3D-printing capabilities into their logistics operations. They sought an investment that could create a sustainable ecosystem through partnerships and capabilities—they wanted a digital platform.

UPS invested in a 3D print start-up called Fast Radius (FR). The firm had taken three funding rounds overall: Seed (2016), Series A (2017), and Series B (2019). UPS liked what it saw with FR's strategy, making a total commitment of $44M across the funding series. FR CEO Lou Rassey is a manufacturing guy at heart. With an MIT engineering degree and several years of running McKinsey's manufacturing practice, he was managing a VC firm when UPS recruited him during FR's Series A round.

UPS no doubt sees an opportunity in contract manufacturing (CM)—customers with centralized ordering and massive quantity demands. UPS serves over seven million customers with smaller orders, whereas CMs have a smaller number of customers with much larger order sizes. As a result, CM's challenges in design, processing, salesforce, and customer service are different from traditional manufacturing.

Partnering with FR, UPS is sticking its corporate toe into the water of on-demand manufacturing, considering local and regional nodes with potentially 50 to 100 small "factories" among its many sites.

There's nothing preventing UPS from doing the same with other small 3D-printing firms if it so chooses.

But this is no panacea. It can be difficult to maintain quality control across multiple systems in a distributed landscape. Numerous factors affect product outcome and performance characteristics—temperature, humidity, raw materials suppliers, and packaging, to name but a few. A part designed in a Chicago winter must keep its designed characteristics when printed in a South Florida summer. Who owns that risk? UPS likely believed they did and perhaps is concerned about the difficulties in copying a single process at multiple locations.

Design file integrity is a concern among additive manufacturing customers, something the largely open-source software of industrial 3D printers isn't designed to protect. UPS has little experience in securing other company's intellectual property (IP). (A group of university researchers hacked a 3D printer of drone parts and the sabotaged design file caused a drone to fail at altitude.[8])

Post processing is another area where UPS might have a steep learning curve. Many 3D-printing parts require additional work after the initial printing is done. This can be especially true with metal parts, which can be dangerously sharp. Again, who provides the quality control on such manufacturing? UPS's workforce of delivery drivers and warehouse loaders are not materials scientists.

Cost structures change when value-add activity changes raw material into finished product. UPS might also be on the hook for packaging too, no matter how short-lived the part's journey might be. They may handle consumer packages in their retail stores, but not industrial parts at warehouse locations. These are unfamiliar costs in risk management, quality control, and chain of custody.

If UPS becomes more of a manufacturer than shipper, warehouse sites near raw materials production might not be anywhere near customers for finished products based on that raw material. That might negate any "just-in-time" manufacturing advantage, requiring semitrucks to deliver to secondary warehouse locations for parts to be placed on local delivery vehicles.

Alternatively, UPS could eliminate the warehouse and local delivery issues by printing directly on a customer's site, given enough demand.

That might require UPS/FR employees to manage the process at a customer's facility. But these are more likely to be white-collar professionals, technicians in Information Technology or material science engineers, making for very different personnel costs.

This has been a great learning experience for UPS. How do they guarantee the validity of a data file? What are the counterfeiting risks for high margin parts? Who owns the data file risk, both in design and file integrity? How would they test and validate complex one-off products? The company continues to explore these and many other questions through this unique investment with a start-up company.

Preference Model

In 2016, Adidas launched their first robotics manufacturing site in Ansbach, Germany, near their Bavarian corporate headquarters. A second site opened in the United States in Atlanta in 2017. As with the UPS model above, the thinking was to locate manufacturing as close to the customer as possible.

Known as a *SpeedFactory*, the two locations blended advanced robotics and 3D-printing technologies in unique ways. Adidas also experimented with a revolutionary popup store in a Berlin shopping mall. Unglamorously called a *StoreFactory*, the site produced a single product: Machine-knit wool sweaters, made to order right there behind a glass partition.

Designed by the customer, who then had their body scanned by a computer for sizing, they received their bespoke sweater in a couple of hours. It was a groundbreaking experiment in digital design, robotic automation, localized manufacturing, and personalized products.[9] If *StoreFactory* was the model, *SpeedFactory* was the scale up.

The name was no coincidence, as the strategy was to speed up the company's reactions to market demand. The first shoes rolled out in September 2016 and were called *Futurecraft M.FG*, as in "Made For Germany." This localized customization was not simply geographic—the company envisioned similar customizations for everything from big city marathons to the Olympic Games.

Part of this automation was in the form of 3D printed soles by a start-up called Carbon.[10] The desired combination of elasticity and durability Adidas wanted required a lattice structure so complex it could only be manufactured via 3D printing. Combining Carbon's expertise with several separate robotic components, the *SpeedFactory* was a showcase of technologies. A shoe taking several weeks to produce in Asia could be made in the *SpeedFactory* in five hours.[11]

But that complexity created other problems. Adidas makes hundreds of millions of shoes per year—at best, additive manufacturing would only be able to produce a small fraction of this—less than 1 percent.[12] So while mass customization looks good on paper, in reality additive technologies remain labor intensive, the very problem Adidas was hoping it would solve. As with UPS previously, the at-scale labor costs were discouraging.

After a couple of years of operation, Adidas announced in 2019 it was closing both *SpeedFactory* locations, though it would continue to work in 3D print technologies with Oechsler, a German specialist in injection molding who operated the factories under contract.

Adidas is not alone. Competitor Nike has several patents for 3D printed shoe components. In 2016, the Investor's Business Daily ran a story about Nike having more patents that year than Lockheed, Ford Motor Company, or Pfizer.[13] Shoes are a cutthroat business, where even a minor improvement in cost structure can rapidly scale to a significant improvement to both revenue and profits.

Laser cutting of the materials versus hand cutting, automated gluing versus stitching, and other innovations are intended to eliminate overhead costs and underlying bottlenecks. 3D printing will continue to make inroads into these component areas as robotics technology morphs into a plug-n-play model for the assembly process.

One thing Adidas proved was the digital platform for such an undertaking can be done at scale among multiple customers and suppliers. The learning curve remains steep, but Adidas and Nike are making these early bets on the technology to lead the change rather than follow it. These digital platforms are causing traditional manufacturing to catch up to where innovative start-ups like Carbon are impatiently waiting.

Supply Chain Drivers

The disruption to our supply chain during the Covid-19 pandemic has been pronounced. Ships were stacked up outside the Ports of Los Angeles and Long Beach. Trucking firms were trying to extend the available hours their drivers can be behind the wheel to move products to the interior of the country rapidly. The White House created a Task Force to address the problem. But those efforts are still not moving fast enough.

With their supply chain as backed up as everyone else's, energy giant Chevron chose to go in a different direction. Unable to get key replacement parts it required for a $55B project in Australia, it approached a Sydney-based 3D print start-up called AdditiveNow.[14]

The company didn't simply deliver the parts on time—they so impressed the Chevron team that the company decided to license AdditiveNow's IP. Such demand exists across the oil and gas industry. Italian 3D print company Roboze fortuitously opened an office in Houston just before the pandemic hit.[15] It has been inundated with requests from the petroleum industry to provide parts otherwise unavailable.

The levers detailed in the examples—storage versus speed versus shipping—continue to drive new customers to 3D print start-ups, who continue to develop new technologies for delivering more than just products or services. They are delivering solutions!

CHAPTER 15

Joint Research With Colleges/Universities

Big companies looking for start-up opportunities should also consider partnering with universities. These can be anything from a local community college-based student incubator to distinguished research universities anywhere in the world. Consider how your company's standing might compare once you're associated with a new start-up coming out of Stanford or Carnegie Mellon? Imagine walking through those hallowed halls on a regular basis, looking at what the best minds in the world are working on.

I was previously a delegate for a prior employer's membership in MIT's Media Lab (Figure 15.1). Twice a year we'd go up to Boston for members-only presentations on what faculty and students were working on. Members had first crack at licensing this research, and as American Express used to remind us *Membership Has Its Privileges!* I was always impressed by the creativity, innovation, and focus on real-world applications the faculty and students presented.

MIT Media Lab is a research laboratory spun out from the School of Architecture. With a current annual budget of ~$80M, their research draws on technology, media, science, art, and design; it is among the most unique academic facilities in the nation.[1] Funding comes largely from corporate sponsorships spread across a range of general themes. Government institutions like the National Science Foundation and Defense Advanced Research Projects Agency (DARPA) fund more traditional project-based research.

Operating on a subscription-like model, sponsoring companies share the Media Lab's intellectual property (IP) without license fees or royalties. Companies not on the subscription model cannot use the lab's newly developed IP for two years, creating a wonderful incentive to renew the

Figure 15.1 *The author on an autonomous bike at the MIT Media Lab*

annual subscription. The lab acquires around 20 new patents annually from its research.

Though not the only measure of academic performance, patents are a much easier metric to quantify than other sources of IP creation as their application and issuance are controlled (and published) by the federal government. As such, schools with especially large IP successes are happy to show them off and use them to attract corporate sponsors of their research.

While MIT has an established brand, there are a significant number of schools that do equally impressive work but simply don't have the cache or subscription model innovation. But what they do have is the same ability to create Joint Research Agreements to pursue patent protection in concert with corporate partners or start-up firms.

The 2013 America Invents Act, or AIA, was the most significant update to United States patent law in almost 50 years. First, and perhaps most meaningfully for inventors, was switching U.S. policy from a *first-to-invent* (FTI) posture to the same *first-to-file* (FTF) posture the rest of the world already followed.

This means inventorship is a race to file at the patent office. Proving when and how, or even where, an inventor conceived of new product or service is largely moot. What matters is getting the idea documented and filed, by receiving a receipt from the Office with a registration number. With that, protecting the idea is official.

Joint Research Agreements were an additional enhancement created by the AIA. Inventors needed a way to do expensive, complicated, time-sensitive, and just plain difficult research with larger organizations that could provide funding, expertise, facilities, and market access. But many, particularly poorly funded start-ups, were justifiably concerned about sharing their next-generation ideas with potential partners who were more than capable of stealing these innovations out from under them.

The new law creates a common ownership of IP when the owners enter into a Joint Research Agreement. This is important, because any unpublished subject matter disclosed among the partners is no longer prior art for any newly created innovation. The three parameters that must be met are:

1. A written (contract) agreement was in effect on *or before* the effective filing date of the claimed invention resulting from the partnership.
2. The claimed invention was made because of activities undertaken within the scope of the joint research agreement.
3. The patent application discloses (or is amended to disclose) the names of the inventors that were a party to the agreement.

A bunch of legalese? Yes. Important? Absolutely!

What we have here is a framework that allows us to do a wide variety of things with a partnering organization, and in some ways makes otherwise difficult to-work-with organizations (like universities and corporations) attractive for start-up companies.

First off, entering into Joint Research Agreements opens up some of the unpublished inventions a corporation or university might have sitting around. Some of it was possibly developed to a certain point at one time or another, but a tremendous amount is also pushed aside, considered too small an opportunity, or simply abandoned when its internal champion retires or moves on.

The first bullet point shown earlier clears that prior art from being an impediment to an improvement a young start-up might have over a previous technology, product, or service. Because that corporate or academic IP owner is now party to this new joint research, they are effectively providing a "get out of jail free" card to a start-up who would otherwise be estopped from developing the technology any further. The unpublished prior art is no longer an obstacle.

This has been great for universities, many of whom have been pushing patents for years with little (and sometimes no) commercialization of the technology after the patent issues. By partnering with a young start-up, many otherwise unknown innovations are now a useful stake in the commercialization game. Partnering can be as much or as little as the university wishes it to be.

Both corporate and academic partnerships can be done very cost-effectively, minimizing any out-of-pocket expenses on this prior art. Start-ups taking their innovation ideas simply need the past product or service cleared—once that is done under the contractual agreement, they are free to develop. The corporate or academic partner can be compensated if the technology turns into something new and commercialized.

This is where a lot of big companies and universities first begin their work with start-ups. Corporate entities typically have the legal departments necessary to draft up such documents, and depending on how the deal is structured, can even offer their counsel to the start-ups in filing any follow-up patents from the new technology. This can be a relatively easy, nonfinancial contribution to the partnership.

Universities don't generally have large legal departments, but they will often have spaces. Not formal incubators per se, but certainly lab or shop spaces where a new start-up can iterate on an idea using the university's prior art and take it another step or two further in development. What the university lacks in legal expertise can be more than made up for with space and technical consulting.

This is very cost effective for start-ups. While coworking spaces are multiplying rapidly around the country, wet labs and prototyping shops remain a significant cost. Lab spaces generally require hardy chemical-resistant surfaces, ventilated air handling systems, and proper waste disposal protocols. All of these require not just capital outlay and maintenance, they are also highly regulated. Numerous government agencies track and inspect such facilities and they require professional management.

Unfortunately, maker spaces aren't much better. They don't have the biosafety hazard or chemical disposal requirements of laboratories, but they do tend to have high fixed costs in tools and machinery. Industrial 3D printers can run into hundreds of thousands of dollars each, while cutting torches and welding equipment similarly requires a skilled set of hands to operate.

Companies and schools already spending money on such facilities may find ways to allocate parts of these costs by making them available to start-up firms. This is a great way to ease into start-up partnerships in a controlled way, moving into joint research agreements down the road as leaders get more comfortable in how the relationships progress. Fortunately, there are numerous examples of such programs doing great things.

The Regional Analytical Chemistry (RAChel) Laboratory at the University of North Carolina at Charlotte has been around for over 20 years. Operating like a small start-up itself, the lab offers analytical services to start-ups and big corporations in evaluating competitor formulations and products.[2] Again, the nuclear magnetic resonance spectronomy, liquid and gas chromatography, and similarly specialized tools are cost effective when billed out by the hour or project.

But this is not just for start-ups. Corporations stalled on products that can't hit a required internal rate of return to justify further development can instead generate small revenue streams to devote to other projects by partnering with or contracting out to university entities like this. In doing so, it's not uncommon for partners to later realize they've discovered or created something that has more market value than when they began. From such a partnership, new start-ups are created.

City and county development offices can be another great resource for introducing would-be start-up entrepreneurs with corporate or academic partners. Economic Development offices hear from budding entrepreneurs regularly and know which local organizations are actively looking for partnership opportunities and which ones aren't. A quick call or cup of coffee with economic development officials is time well spent, as their goals for more local companies and jobs are aligned with yours. But the opportunities don't end there. Open the aperture a bit wider.

The U.S. Space Force, launched in late 2019, is America's newest military command.[3] Despite their young age (or perhaps because of it), they are looking to partner with entrepreneurs! They've set aside $32M in funding for start-ups and small businesses.[4] These start-ups cross a range of technologies and innovations: propulsion systems, satellite communications, navigation technology, advanced cameras and optics, autonomous control systems, and medical advancements for space application.

Big oil companies are finding new ways to partner with start-ups to tackle problems like climate change. A Sweden-based start-up called Liquid Wind captures CO2 emissions to create methanol for the shipping industry.[5] Chevron and Occidental have backed a British start-up called Carbon Engineering for removing carbon dioxide directly from the atmosphere.[6] BP and Shell have bolstered their corporate venture capital groups to focus on low carbon energy start-ups.[7]

Why all the interest in carbon trading? Two reasons—one, it is ripe for disruption, which is what start-ups typically excel at. And two, the opportunity is forecast to become massive. The market for carbon credits is an impressive $268B today.[8] The energy consulting firm Wood McKenzie expects that number to rocket up to $22T by 2050. When there is massive change, rapid development, or new technologies at play, start-ups are generally better positioned to adjust to them.

Sometimes carbon tracking segues in with a corporation's other technology interests. Agriculture giant Archer Daniels invested in Farmers Business Network, a start-up tracking the carbon trail of crops from the moment they're planted.[9] Kellogg's cereal has several start-up partnerships and investments, all food oriented, that align with their corporate strategy.[10] Big food and beverage companies only allocate 1 to 2 percent of their budget to R&D, so this is a good way to maximize innovation.

UPS similarly has a range of internal, external, and extended concept start-ups they are supporting.[11] As with Kellogg's, each is selected based on a set of key corporate interests, here it is supply chain and logistics. Both companies use a range of tools from joint research agreements to direct investments into start-ups creating new technologies.

Carbon footprint, supply chain, logistics, and similar underlying infrastructure technologies are not sexy. Because this type of back-office function is not a primary driver for revenue, they can be difficult to secure venture capital funding for them. That makes them perfect for university research and the start-ups that spin out of them.

Environmental Science, chemistry, and applied mathematics have just as many dedicated researchers as engineering, medicine, and computer science. Universities that have perhaps not been cutting edge in spinning off start-ups will find willing corporate partners to develop behind-the-scenes solutions to these and many other problems. The universities don't need to be brand names or have shiny new buildings. All they need is willing, dedicated researchers and a desire to partner with big companies to solve difficult problems. Another win–win opportunity!

Congratulations

You're Now One of Us!

Well, guess what? That sort of just snuck on up you, didn't it?

If you've gotten all the way to here without yelling *"this guy is nuts!"* then you're a kindred spirit. You are trying to build something in your corporation that didn't exist before. A new company within a company.

You're an *intra*preneur!

Take a moment, let it sink in. Yes, the task in front of you is considerable. There will be many naysayers, so count on that. There will be those who cross their fingers and pray to the start-up gods that you fail miserably. But don't let that dissuade you.

Instead, think of all the thought-leading companies that you can now associate yourself with. Accountants, engineers, and graphic artists don't often get to rub shoulders with the premiere technology or industrial giants such as Apple, Google, or UPS. But you will!

You'll not only have reason to meet many of these people, you'll have opportunities to pick their brains and potentially partner together on new innovations. Remember: incubators, accelerators, and venture financing are strategic investments, not corporate get-rich-quick schemes, so be in it for the long haul!

Fortunately or unfortunately, large corporations are sitting on unprecedented amounts of cash. With supply chain issues restricting access to high-priced equipment and Human Resources Departments unable to hire (or keep) staff for long periods, CFOs find themselves with an abundance of money. Many of them are using the funds to buy back their own shares.[1]

But that is shortsighted thinking! If investing through in-house R&D is not viable due to the same supply chain and hiring issues, why not instead take advantage of the imperfect opportunity and invest in start-up companies to leapfrog the competition? Certainly many of them are considering the same, so the competition for advanced ideas and disruptive technologies may well soon be intense. Five years from now, which will make shareholders happy—buying stock to hold the current price, or investing in future products and services to drive that price higher?

So find those outside opportunities, or create a few internal ones as well, knowing that start-up funding is no longer a problem that will stop you. You're in the best negotiating position you could possibly hope for.

Welcome to the first day of your new future!

TJW

Notes

Introduction

1. Graham (2021).

Chapter 1

1. Monroe (2013).
2. Sisario (2019).
3. Monroe (2013).
4. Kotash (2022).
5. Monroe (2013).
6. Larson (2011).
7. Bass (1979).
8. Rupertneve.com Editors (2021).
9. Rupertneve.com Editors (2021).
10. Stokes (2021).
11. Monroe (2013).
12. Monroe (2013).
13. Hoffman (1978).
14. Chen (2020).
15. Eisen (2019).
16. Fest (2019).
17. Siegel (2011).
18. Steele (2020).
19. Steele (2021).

Chapter 2

1. The Economist (2017).
2. Bernstein and Kevin (2015).
3. Greene (2020).
4. Barro (2019).

5. The Editorial Board (2019).

6. Garner (2019).

7. Miranda (2021).

8. Fogden (2018).

9. Susskind and Sarah (1999).

10. Heater (2021).

11. Davidson (2011).

12. Shu (2018).

13. Garcia (2021).

14. PR Newswire (2018).

15. UBS Research Note (2018).

Chapter 3

1. Kurlyandchik (2019).

2. Bousquette (2022).

3. Miller (2016).

4. Weekly (2020).

5. Tiffany (2021).

6. Gavetti (2004).

Chapter 4

1. PMTS.com (2019).

2. Newhouse (2019).

3. Feldman (2020).

Chapter 5

1. Korosec (2020).

2. Xcelerator (2021).

3. Amazon.com (2021).

4. Mattioli (2020).

5. M12 Editors (n.d.).

6. Website Editors (n.d.).

7. Website Editors (n.d.).
8. Riley (2021).
9. Kane (2016).
10. Sorrentino, Nick, and Frank (2015).
11. Calhoun (2019).
12. Abrahamson (2015).
13. Stanford (2022), p. 3.
14. Go (2010).
15. Newcomer (2015).
16. Levi (2014).
17. Al-Heeti (2020).
18. Calhoun (2019).
19. Case (2021).
20. Loten (2020).
21. Pitchbook (2019).
22. Allyn (2021).
23. Bezos (2019).
24. Stillman (2020).
25. Boitnott (2016).
26. Demmitt (2019).

Chapter 6

1. Waters (1997).
2. Geller and Danya (2011).
3. Editorial Staff (2021).
4. Wray (2021).

Chapter 7

1. Govindarajan and Immelt (2019).
2. Sharma (2021).
3. Dowd (2021).
4. Ernst & Young (2016), p. 17.
5. Ernst & Young (2016), p. 16.

6. Ernst & Young (2016), p. 5.
7. Contributor (2015).
8. Noventum & Aston Business School (2017).
9. Statista (2021).
10. The United Nations (2014).
11. Hertzberg (2018).
12. Noventum & Aston Business School (2017).

Chapter 8

1. The Drucker Institute (2011).
2. PR Newswire (2019).
3. Johnson (2018).
4. Bell (2018).
5. Flinders (2017).
6. Liao (2019).
7. Fung (2016).
8. Borakove (2018).

Chapter 9

1. Tampa Bay Buccaneers Facebook Page (n.d.).
2. Hall (2021).
3. Biggs (2015).
4. Savitz (2020).
5. Opelka (2021).
6. Brown and Tanya (2013).
7. Grant (2021).
8. Tilley (2020).
9. Schultz (2021).
10. Sindreu (2021).
11. Gryta and Cara (2020).
12. Azoluay, Benjamin, Daniel, and Javier (2018).
13. Soper (2019).
14. Kerruish and Matt (2019).
15. White House Editors (n.d.).
16. Clover (2021).

Chapter 10

1. Abramovitch (2019).
2. Jurgensen (2019).
3. Grynbaum, Nicole, and Julia (2021).
4. Flint and Denny (2022).
5. Bell (2018).
6. Shepherd (2020).
7. May (2016).

Chapter 11

1. Alexander (2019).
2. Day (2019).
3. O'Brien (2018).
4. Tilley (2015).
5. Tilley (2015).
6. O'Brien (2018).
7. Burgett (2019).
8. Lentino (2019).
9. Syed (2019).
10. Hassan (2017).
11. Duke Today Staff (2015).
12. Byron (2019).
13. GE Staff (2019).
14. Ekman (2019).
15. Editors (2019 [2022]).
16. Frangoul (2019).
17. Fried and Keven (2019).
18. Hawkins (2019).
19. Davies (2019).
20. Salesky (2017).
21. Wiggers (2018).
22. Linder (2019).
23. Carlier (2022).
24. Hyatt (2018).
25. Korosec (2019).

26. Vincent (2019).

27. Kormehl (2020).

28. Christian (2020).

29. Eadicicco (2020).

30. Campbell (2019).

31. Fisher (2019).

32. Matney (2019).

33. Strange (2019).

34. Korosec (2021).

35. Bellan (2021).

36. Goldstein (2021).

Chapter 12

1. McGrath (2006).

2. Staley (2017).

3. Tiwary (2019).

4. IMPACT Editors (2017).

5. Burch (2017).

6. Automotive World (2020).

7. Boston Consulting Group (2020).

8. Colias (2021).

9. Schartau and Gianluigi (2021).

10. Hardman and Gil (2021).

11. Boston (2019).

12. Maurer (2019).

13. Sindreu (2021).

14. Eistenstein (2019).

15. Wren (2019).

16. Boston (2019).

17. Lambert (2020).

18. Colias (2020).

19. Colias (2020).

20. Motavalli (2020).

21. Brennan (2020).

22. Crowe (2020).

23. Webb (2019).

24. The BBC (2021).
25. Dent (2021).
26. Olson (2019).
27. TVA Editors (n.d.).
28. Staff Reporter (2021).
29. Davis (2021).
30. Tennessee (2021).
31. DET Editors (2019).

Chapter 13

1. Norton (2017).
2. Wong (2017).
3. Perez (2017).
4. Needleman (2017).
5. Yadron (2015).
6. Yadron (2015).
7. Needleman (2017).
8. Khandwelwal (2019).
9. Tassi (2017).
10. Hill (2012).
11. Reece and Christopher (n.d.).
12. Tran (2017).
13. Grove (2017).
14. Kesslar (2020).
15. Castillo (2015).
16. Allen (2019).
17. Pagliery (2015).
18. Moore (2014).
19. Vidino, Lewis, and Mines (2020).
20. The World Service (2019).
21. Hassan (2019).

Chapter 14

1. Cusumano, Annabelle, and David (2018).
2. Stone (2007).

3. USG (2017).

4. Jackson (2017).

5. Editorial Staff (n.d.).

6. Cooper (2017).

7. Cap Gemini Research Institute (2019).

8. Forrest (2016).

9. Hijano (2017).

10. Molitch-Hou (2017).

11. Williams (2017).

12. Smith (2019).

13. Low (2016).

14. Condie (2021).

15. Miranda (2020).

Chapter 15

1. MIT Editors (2018).

2. UNCC Editors (n.d.).

3. US Space Force Editors (n.d.).

4. Erwin (2021).

5. Thorne (2011).

6. Brigham (2019).

7. McFarlane (2015).

8. Toplensky (2021).

9. Maltais (2021).

10. 1894.com Editors (n.d.).

11. UPS.com Editors (2021).

Congratulations: You're Now One of Us!

1. Trentman and Mark (2021).

References

1894.com Editors. n.d. "The Destination for Ideas." Kellogg's Eighteen94 Capital, LLC. Last updated 2022. www.1894capital.com/en_US/home.html

Abrahamson, S. December 08, 2015. "The Micro VCs Are Coming." *Mattermark*.

Abramovitch, S. May 20, 2019. "James Holzhaeur Returns to 'Jeopardy!' as Insiders Reveal Financial Details of a Record Streak." *The Hollywood Reporter*.

Alexander, J. May 13, 2019. "Canon and Nikon Report Sales Drop of Over 17% Since Last Year." *Fstoppers*.

Al-Heeti, A. February 12, 2020. "Silicon Valley Continues Losing People as Costs Rise, Report Says." *C/net*.

Allen, K. October 27, 2019. "Family of Slain ISIS Hostage Kayla Mueller Says They Secretly Met With Her Captors in Iraq." *ABC News*.

Allyn, B. July 05, 2021. "Jeff Bezos Built Amazon 27 Years Ago. He Now Steps Down as CEO at Critical Time." *NPR*.

Amazon.com. December 2021. Amazon Jobs.

Automotive World. June 03, 2020. "Class # 5 of Volkswagen's Incubator Programme: Five Startup Make a Virtual Start to the Next Round."

Azoluay, P., B. Jones, D. Kim, and J. Miranda. July 11, 2018. "Research: The Average Age of a Successful Startup Founder is 45." *The Harvard Business Review*.

Barro, J. February 22, 2019. "What We Did and Didn't Learn From the Failed Amazon-Queens Deal." *New York Magazine*. Intelligencer.

Bass, D. 1979. "Pro Session—The Studio As Compositional Tool." *Downbeat*.

Bell, K. June 12, 2018. "Instagram Is Proof Shameless Copying Pays Off." *Mashable*.

Bell, T. February 27, 2018. "Can Telemedicine Be Both Cost Efficient and High Quality?" US News and World Report.

Bellan, R. November 10, 2021. "Foxconn Buys Lordstown Motors' Ohio Factory for $230M, Plans to help Produce Endurance Electric Pickup." *Techcrunch*.

Bernstein, J. and K. Hasset. April 2015. "Unlocking Private Capital to Facilitate Economic Growth in Distressed Areas." *The American Enterprise Institute*.

Bezos, J. April 11, 2019. "2018 Letter to Shareholders." *Amazon.com*.

Biggs, T. March 24, 2015. "How Atari's Nolan Bushnell Turned Down Steve Jobs' Offer of a Third of Apple at $50,000." *The Sydney Morning News*.

Boitnott, J. April 26, 2016. "6 Alternatives to Silicon Valley With Better Weather Than Portland." *Entrepreneur*.

Borakove, J. July 17, 2018. "In the War for Talent, Your Best Weapon Is Your Current Workforce." *Forbes Magazine.*

Boston Consulting Group. September 17, 2020. "The Economic Impact of Ford and the F-Series."

Boston, W. November 29, 2019. "Daimler Looks to Cut Thousands of Jobs." *The Wall Street Journal.*

Boston, W. October 22, 2019. "Car Parts Supplier Continental to Overhaul Business." *The Wall Street Journal.*

Bousquette, I. March 31, 2022. "Walmart Announces New Tech Hubs in Toronto and Atlanta." *The Wall Street Journal.*

Brennan, R. March 06, 2020. "Electric Vehicles Are Changing the Future of Auto Maintenance." *Techcrunch.*

Brigham, K. June 22, 2019. "Bill Gates and Big Oil Back This Company That's Trying to Solve Climate Change By Sucking CO2 Out of the Air." *CNBC.*

Brown, N. and T. Agrawal. September 03, 2013. "Kodak Emerges From Bankruptcy with Focus on Commercial Printing." *Reuters.*

Burch, B. February 27, 2017. "Jaguar Land Rover Invests in Artificial Intelligence Startup Mycroft." Startland News.

Burgett, G. February 21, 2019. "Light and Sony Team up to Make the Next-Generation of Multi-Camera Smartphones." *Digital Photography Review.*

Byron, E. April 17, 2019. "We Now Live in a World With Customized Shampoo." *The Wall Street Journal.*

Calhoun, L. August 29, 2019. "A VC Expert Explains 3 Inevitable Forces Rebooting Venture Capital Right Now." *Business Insider.*

Campbell, M. September 11, 2019. "Details of Apple's Rumored AR Headset Revealed in iOS 13 GM." *Apple Insider.*

Cap Gemini Research Institute. 2019. "The Last Mile Delivery Challenge." *Cap Gemini.*

Carlier, M. January 10, 2022. "Number of Tesla Vehicles Delivered Worldwide From 1st Quarter 2016 to 4th Quarter 2021." *Statista.*

Case, S. July 13, 2021. "Innovation Moves to Middle America." *The Wall Street Journal.*

Castillo, M. January 12, 2015. "Leaked Documents: Bernie Madoff Convicted Thanks to Mysterious Palantir Technology." *American Cities Business Journals.*

Chen, J.. 2020. "What Is a Bowie Bond." *Investopedia.*

Christian, R. October 06, 2020. "Foxconn to Finish Microled AR Smart Glasses in 2022." *Channel News Australia.*

Clover, J. July 16, 2021. "Apple Watch Chief Kevin Lynch to Work on Apple Car Development." *Mac Rumors.*

Colias, M. January 27, 2020. "GM Picks Detroit Factory to Build Driverless Shuttle, Electric Trucks." *The Wall Street Journal.*

Colias, M. June 25, 2020. "The 2021 Ford F-150 Aims to Double as a Rolling Office." *The Wall Street Journal.*

Colias, M. August 01, 2021. "Ford's Utility Man Drives Its Commercial-Vehicle Strategy." *The Wall Street Journal.*

Condie, S. November 11, 2021. "Energy Companies Turn to 3D Printing to Bypass Snarled Supply Chains." *The Wall Street Journal.*

Contributor. February 13, 2015. "How STEEP and STEEPLE Analysis Help in Business." *Pestle Analysis.*

Cooper, D. September 14, 2017. "How Electroloom's Clothes-Printing Revolution Died." *Engadget.*

Crowe, R. November 09, 2020. "SwRI Hacks Electric Vehicle Charting to Demonstrate Cybersecurity Vulnerabilities." *Science Magazine.*

Cusumano, M., A. Gawer, and D. Yoffie. 2018. *The Business of Platforms.* New York, NY: HarperCollins.

Davidson, P. August 11, 2011. "Move Here, Get Paid: Small Towns Offer Up to $20K Just to Get You to Live There, Work Remotely." *The USA Today.*

Davies, A. May 23, 2019. "Self Driving Startup Aurora Buys Seed Sensing Lidar Company." *Wired.*

Davis, C. September 29, 2021. "How Tennessee Became the Top Electric Car Producers in the Southeast." *News Channel 5, Nashville.*

Day, A. April 29, 2019. "Canon's Dramatic Drop in Sales is a Sign of Something Much More Ominous for Photographers." *Fstoppers.*

Demmitt, J. April 07, 2019. "Startup Checkup: Roanoke, Blacksburg Short on Cash to Launch Startups." *The Roanoke Times.*

Dent, S. September 17, 2021. "Rolls Royce All Electric Aircraft Competes 15 Minute Maiden Voyage." *Techcrunch.*

DET Editors. January 2019. "Roadmap" Institute for a Secure and Sustainable Environment, Drive Electric TN." https://driveelectrictn.org/wp-content/uploads/2019/08/Roadmap_for_Electric_Vehicles_in_Tennessee_Report.pdf

Dowd, K. November 14, 2021. "Death to Conglomerates: GE, J&J, and Toshiba All Reveal Plans to Break Themselves Up." *Forbes.*

Duke Today Staff. October 14, 2015. "Duke Launches Autism Research App." *Duke Today.*

Eadicicco, L. July 10, 2020. "Apple Is Reportedly Producing Lenses for What Could Be Its Next Major Product: An Augmented Reality Headset." *Business Insider.*

Editorial Staff. June 16, 2021. "Macron Pushes for 10 €100BIL Tech Companies by 2030." *Engineering and Technology.*

Editorial Staff. n.d. "What Was Matterfab?." *Failory.com.* www.failory.com/cemetery/matterfab

Editors. October 27, 2019. "Telemedicine Catches on: Changes in the Utilization of Telemedicine Services During Covid the Covid 19 Pandemic." *American Journal of Managed Care*, Volume 28, Issue 1, January 2022.

Eisen, B. August 08, 2019. "Adele, Auto Parts and Massages: Debt Deals Dress Up Unusual Assets." *The Wall Street Journal.*

Eistenstein, P. October 03, 2019. "Electric Vehicles Pose 'Real Risk' for Autoworkers, With Fewer Parts—And Jobs—Required." *The Wall Street Journal.*

Ekman, P. June 05, 2019. "The Dangers of Reading Micro Expressions." *Psychology Today.*

Ernst & Young. 2016. *The Upside of Disruption: Megatrends Shaping 2016 and Beyond,* p. 5, 16, 17.

Erwin, S. August 20, 2021. "Space Force Awards $32 Million in Contracts to Startups and Small Businesses." *Space News.*

Feldman, A. July 30, 2020. "Why 40 North Ventures Bought GE Ventures' Stakes in 11 Industrial Startups." *Forbes Magazine.*

Fest, G. May 2019. "Massage Envy Turns to Whole Biz ABS for Debt Refinancing." *American Banker.* Asset Securitization Report.

Fisher, C. September 13, 2019. "Another AR Headset Startup Closes Its Doors." *Engadget.*

Flinders, K. October 31, 2017. "Mobile Software Is Replacing Bank Branches and Cash as Youngsters Prefer Apps." *Computer Weekly.*

Flint, J. and D. Jacob. April 19, 2022. "Netflix Explores a Version With Ads as Subscriber Base Shrinks." *The Wall Street Journal.*

Fogden, T. August 2018. "Why Chattanooga Has the Fastest Internet in the US." *Tech.Co.*

Forrest, C. October 20, 2016. "3D Printing Hack: Researchers Crash Drone With Sabotaged Propeller." *TechRepublic.*

Frangoul, A. September 24, 2019. "Hyundai and Aptiv to Set Up $4 Billion Autonomous Driving Joint Venture." *CNBC.*

Fried, I. and K. Waddell. June 25, 2019. "Apple Acquires Self Driving Startup Drive.AI." *Axios.*

Fung, E. November 22, 2016. "Dear Tenant: Your Uber Is Here." *The Wall Street Journal.*

Garcia, T. March 31, 2021. "Lululemon Sees Big Potential in Mirror, But Investments Drive Guidance Lower." *MarketWatch.*

Garner, M. August 28, 2019. "Worried About Amazon Taking Your Talent? AllianceBernstein's CEO Isn't." *Nashville Business Journal.* American Cities Business Journals.

Gavetti, G., R. Henderson, and S. Giorgi. November 2004. "Kodak and the Digital Revolution." *The Harvard Business School.*

GE Staff. September 12, 2019. "GE Healthcare Receives FDA Clearance of First Artificial Intelligence Algorithms Embedded On-Device to Prioritize Critical Chest X-ray Review." *GE Healthcare.*

Geller, D. and D. Goldfine. 2011. *Something Ventured.* New York, NY: Zeitgeist Films.

Go, R. July 12, 2010. "How Micro-VCs Invest (And How They Compare to Traditional VCs)." *Business Insider.*

Goldstein, M., L. Hirsch, and N.E. Boudette. June 14, 2021. "Lordstown, Truck Maker That Can't Afford to Make Trucks, Is on the Brink." *The New York Times.*

Govindarajan, V. and I. Jeffrey. March 12, 2019. "The Only Way Manufacturers Can Survive." *MIT Sloan Management Review.*

Grabham, D. 16 June 2021. "Apple's Tim Cook: We Do It All." *Pocket-Lint.*

Grant, C. April 02, 2021. "To Spin or Not to Spin? Disposals Crete Fortunes and Headaches." *The Wall Street Journal.*

Greene, D. January 13, 2020. "Foxconn Promised 13,000 Jobs to Wisconsin. Where Are They?" *National Public Radio.* NPR/WUSF.

Grove, T., J. Barnes, and D. Hinshaw. October 04, 2017. "Russia Targets NATO Solider Smartphones, Western Officials Say." *The Wall Street Journal.*

Grynbaum, M.M., N. Sperling, and J. Jacobs. August 31, 2021. "Mike Richards Is Out as 'Jeopardy!' Executive Producer." *The New York Times.*

Gryta, T. and C. Lombardo. May 27, 2020. "GE Exits Lightbulb Business It Pioneered." *The Wall Street Journal.*

Hall, J. July 26, 2021. "Jilted Tom Brady on Team Who Chose Another QB: 'They Know Who They Are'." *Fox Sports Radio.*

Hardman, S. and G. Tal. April 26, 2021. "Understanding Discontinuance Among California's Electric Vehicle Owners." NATURE ENERGY. www.nature.com/articles/s41560-021-00814-9

Hassan, J. October 30, 2019. "Kayla Mueller's Parents Call Baghdadi Raid Named for Their Slain Daughter an 'Amazing Gift'." *The Washington Post.*

Hassan, M. February 07, 2017. "Is Biometric Technology The 'Go To' Solution to Prevent Bank Fraud?." *M2SYS.*

Hawkins, A. April 24, 2019. "It's Elon Musk Vs Everyone Else In the Race for Fully Driverless Cars." *The Verge.*

Heater, B. July 02, 2021. "CMU's President Discusses How Pittsburgh is Building—and Retaining—High Tech Startups." *TechCrunch.com.*

Hertzberg, R. June 08, 2018. "Musician Jack Johnson Wages War on Ocean Plastic." *National Geographic Society.*

Hijano, E. November 29, 2017. "Inside Adidas' Robot-Powered, ON-Demand Sneaker Factory." *Wired.*

Hill, K. February 16, 2012. "How Target Figured Out a Teen Girl Was Pregnant Before Her Father Did." *Forbes.*

Hoffman, R. 1978. *The Startup of You.* New York, NY: Random House.

Hyatt, K. July 12, 2018. "Siemens Mustang Struggles to Self-Drive Up Goodwood Hill." *CNET.*

IMPACT Editors. February 02, 2017. "Welcome to the new Impact Accelerator Website." IMPACT Accelerator. www.impact-accelerator.com/2017/02/

Jackson, B. July 21, 2017. "Oak Ridge Release Details of the U.S. Military's First 3D Printed Submarine." *3D Printing Industry.*

Johnson, S.R. September 25, 2018. "Healthcare Remains Prime Target for Hackers." *Modern Healthcare.*

Jurgensen, J. July 26, 2019. "LeVar Burton Will Guest Host 'Jeopardy!', as One of TV's Most Divisive Hiring Searches Nears an End." *The Wall Street Journal.*

Kane, L. July 13, 2016. "Shark Tank Investor: Entrepreneurs Are the Only People Who Will Work 80 Hours a Week to Avoid Working 40 Hours a Week." *Business Insider.*

Kerruish, S. and M. Maude. 2019. *General Magic.* Gravitas Ventures, DVD.

Kesslar, S. September 30, 2020. "Palantir: The Darling of Secret Services Goes Pubic." *Deutsche Welle.*

Khandwelwal, S. November 07, 2019. "Built In Keylogger Found in MantisTek GK2 Keyboards—Sends Data to China." *The Hacker News.*

Kormehl, L. September 30, 2020. "Apple's Biggest Manufacturer Is Building AR Glasses of Its Own." *Cult of Mac.*

Korosec, K. January 07, 2019. "Autonomous Trucking Startup TuSimple Is Taking 3 to 5 Commercial Trips a Day." *Techcrunch.*

Korosec, K. January 30, 2020. "Techstars Detroit Accelerator Is Shutting Down." *Techcrunch.*

Korosec, K. February 24, 2021. "Apple Supplier Foxconn Reaches Tentative Agreement to Build Fisker's Next Electric Car." *Techcrunch.*

Kotash, K. n.d. "Startup Failure Rate: How Many Startups Fail and Why." *Failory .com.* Last update January 09, 2022.

Kurlyandchik, M. May 08, 2019. "How the Invention of Gatorade Generated Hundreds of Millions in Royalties for the University of Florida." *Celebrity Net Worth.*

Lambert, F. January 17, 2020. "Daimler Announces Upcoming Electric Garbage Truck." *Electrek.*

Larsen, C. 2011. "Rick Springfield Wants Jessie's Girl." *Grammy.com.*

Lentino, A. May 17, 2019. "This Chinese Facial Recognition Startup Can Identify a Person in Seconds." *CNBC.*

Levi, A. January 18, 2014. "Dropbox Value Said to Be $10 Billion in BlackRock Funding." *Bloomberg,* (Subscription). www.bloomberg.com/news/articles/2014-01-18/dropbox-said-to-be-worth-10-billion-in-blackrock-funding

Liao, R. April 16, 2019. "Alibaba Will Let You Find Restaurants and Order Food With Voice in a Car." *Techcrunch.*

Linder, C. August 28, 2019. "Who Owns Lidar?" *Popular Mechanics.*

Loten, A. February 27, 2020. "Cloud Demand Drives Data Center Market to New Records." *The Wall Street Journal.*

Low, E. May 13, 2016. "Why Nike Has More Patents Than Lockheed, Ford, and Pfizer." *Investor's Business Daily.*

M12 Editors. n.d. "Investing in Innovation, Globally." *M12, Microsoft's Venture Fund.*

Maltais, K. November 18, 2021. "ADM Buys Stake in Startup Farmers Business Network." *The Wall Street Journal.*

Matney, L. January 10, 2019. "An AR Glasses Pioneer Collapses." *Techcrunch.*

Mattioli, D. June 23, 2020. "Amazon to Launch $2B Billion Venture Capital Fund to Invest in Clean Energy." *The Wall Street Journal.*

Maurer, M. October 01, 2019. "Auto-Parts Supplier's Incoming CFO to Focus on Revenue Boost for Electrical Business." *The Wall Street Journal.*

May, M. June 01, 2016. "Why Coming Up With Original Ideas Is Actually 'Easier for Your Brain." *Inc Magazine.*

McFarlane, S. August 14, 2015. "Oil Giants Turn to Startups for Low Carbon Energy Ideas." *The Wall Street Journal.*

McGrath, J. June 29, 2006. "GM ECO Admits Killing Electric Car Was a Blunder." *Grist.Org.*

Miller, R. December 29, 2016. "Coca Cola Closes Founders Startup Incubator." *TechCrunch.*

Miranda, J. June 09, 2020. "Italian 3D Printing Company to Set Up US Headquarters in Houston." *Houston Innovation Map.*

Miranda, L. April 05, 2021. "Amazon Is Snapping Disused Shopping Malls and Turning Them Into Fulfillment Centers." *NBC News.*

MIT Editors. Fall 2018. "The MIT Media Lab at a Glance." *MIT Press.*

Molitch-Hou, M. April 07, 2017. "Adidas Uses Carbon's 3D Printing to Mass-Produce Futurecraft 4D Shoes." *Engineering.*

Monroe, M. 2013. *Sound City.* Los Angeles, CA: Gravitas Ventures.

Moore, J. October 03, 2014. "Mosul Seized: Jihadis Loot $429 Million From City's Central Bank to Make ISIS World's Richest Terror Force." *International Business Times.*

Motavalli, J. August 27, 2020. "Soon, the Kitty Litter Will Come by Electric Truck." *The New York Times.*

Needleman, S. January 08, 2017. "How Mobile Games Aim to Keep You Coming Back." *The Wall Street Journal.*

Needleman, S. April 19, 2017. "Videogame 'Add Ons': Billion Dollar Business and Two-Edged Sword." *The Wall Street Journal.*

Newcomer, E. December 03, 2015. "Uber Raises Funding at $62.5 Billion Valuation." *Bloomberg.*

Newhouse, M. November 04, 2019. "GE Ventures to Sell Its Healthcare Venture Investments to Leerink Revelation Partners." *GE.com.*

Norton, S. November 15, 2017. "Era of AI-Powered Cyberattacks Has Started." *The Wall Street Journal.*

Noventum & Aston Business School. 2017. "MEGATRENDS: The Impact of Societal Trends on the Manufacturing Business." London, UK.

O'Brien, J. November 01, 2018. "Exclusive Sneak Peak: The LightCo Is Advancing Computational Photography in Smartphones." *TechBuzz Ireland.*

Olson, P. October 10, 2019. "Dyson, Known for Vacuum Cleaners, Abandons Electric Car Race." *The Wall Street Journal.*

Opelka, G. April 04, 2021. "Xerox Is an Inspiration to Late Bloomers." *The Wall Street Journal.*

Pagliery, J. December 11, 2015. "Inside the $2 Billion ISIS War Machine." *CNN Money.*

Perez, B. June 20, 2017. "The World Spends $109 Billion on Video Games, and the Chinese Are the Biggest Players." *South China Morning Post.*

Pitchbook. January 28, 2019. "18 Charts to Illustrate US VC in 2018."

PMNTS.com. June 13, 2019. "GE Seeks to Unload 100 Startups From Portfolio."

PR Newswire. April 17, 2019. "Lark Health's Diabetes Prevention Program Demonstrates Positive Outcomes in Older Adults." *Lark Health.*

PR Newswire. September 25, 2019. "Foot Locker Inc Announces Strategic Investment in NTWRK."

Reece, A. and C. Danforth. n.d. "Instagram Photos Reveal Predictive Markers of Depression." White Paper. *ARXIV.ORG.*

Riley, C. July 09, 2021. "Automakers Are Tech Companies Now." *CNN Business.*

Rupertneve.com Editors. n.d. "Rupert Neve History." Last update February 12, 2021.

Salesky, B. October 27, 2017. "How Acquiring a Team of LiDAR Experts Strengthens Aro.AI's Self Driving Future." *Ground Truth Autonomy.*

Savitz, E. February 28, 2020. "How Venture Capital Became Intel's Answer to 'Massive Disruption'." *Barron's.*

Schartau, P. and G. Indino. June 18, 2021. "Why EV's Don't Spell Doom for the Aftermarket." *Ernst & Young.*

Schultz, C. July 20, 2021. "EV shocker: Tesla's Software Business Forecast by Morgan Stanley to be More Valuable Than Hardware." *Seeking Alpha.*

Sharma, R. November 10, 2021. "General Electric (GE) Splits Into 3 Companies." *Investopedia.*

Shepherd, M. September 28, 2020. "Stripe vs. Square: How to Choose One for Your Business." *Fundera.*

Shu, C. January 30, 2018. "Virtual Travel Assistant Mezi Acquired by American Express." *TechCrunch.com.*

Siegel, J. October 06, 2011. "When Steve Jobs Got Fired by Apple." *ABC News*.

Sindreu, J. March 05, 2021. "E-Commerce Is a Dangerous Temptation for the Aviation Industry." *The Wall Street Journal*.

Sindreu, J. March 15, 2021. "Are Frequent Flier Miles Really Worth More Than Planes?." *The Wall Street Journal*.

Sisario, B. December 30, 2019. "Jimmy Iovine Knows Music and Tech. Here's Why He's Worried." *The New York Times*.

Smith, O. December 17, 2019. "The Adidas Speedfactory, a Hyped Up Failure or a Supply Chain Success?." *3D Print*.

Soper, T. December 09, 2019. "New Program in Seattle Aims to Help Tech Workers Leaving Companies and Launch Their Own Startups." *GeekWire*.

Sorrentino, T., N. Wiggins, and F. Cicero. November 2015. "Venture Capital Disrupts Itself: Breaking the Concentration Curse." *Cambridge Associates*. Private Investment Series.

Staff Reporter. February 11, 2021. "Volkswagen Recommits to 2022 Electric Vehicle Assembly in Chattanooga Despite Ruling Against Supplier." *The Chattanooga Times Free Press*.

Staley, O. April 07, 2017. "The GM CEO Who Killed the Original Electric Car Is now in the Electric Car Business." *QUARTZ*.

Stanford, K. April 05, 2022. *"Micro-Funding Opportunities." Pitchbook Research Note*, p. 3.

Statista. November 2021. "Headphones."

Steele, A. December 04, 2020. "Stevie Nicks Sells Stake in Songwriting Catalog." *The Wall Street Journal*.

Steele, A. July 30, 2021. "Publisher Buy Stakes From Prince's Heirs in Bid to Steer Singer's Legacy." *The Wall Street Journal*.

Stillman, J. September 03, 2020. "3 Billionaires' Best Advice for Getting Over Your Fear of Failure." *Inc Magazine*.

Stokes, W. February 15, 2021. "He Was the Steve Jobs of Audio: How Rupert Neve Changed the Sound of Music." *The Guardian*.

Stone, B. October 25, 2007. "Microsoft Buy Stake in Facebook." *The New York Times*.

Strange, A. January 09, 2019. "AR Startup Meta Company Shuts Down Amid Asset Foreclosure Sale, Patent Fight, & Executive Departures." *Next Reality News*.

Susskind, L. and S. McKearnen. August 1999. *The Consensus Building Handbook*. New York, NY: Sage Publications.

Syed, S. May 10, 2019. "This Surveillance Camera Can Spot You From 45 KM Away." *Techjuice*.

Tampa Bay Buccaneers Facebook page. n.d. "Tom Brady's Legendary Ring Ceremony Speech." *Facebook*.

Tassi, P. June 08, 2017. "CD Projekt Red Reveals It's Being Blackmailed for Stolen 'Cyberpunk 2077' Files." *Forbes*.

Tennessee Valley Authority. August 25, 2021. "TVA to Convert Half Its Fleet to Electric Vehicles by 2030." *Fuels Fix*.

The BBC. November 20, 2021. "Rolls Royce Says Its All Electric Aircraft 'Is World's Fastest'."

The Drucker Institute. January 14, 2011. "Opportunity in Disguise."

The Economist. October 21, 2017. "Globalization Has Marginalized Many Regions of the World."

The Editorial Board. August 14, 2019. "The Kansas-Missouri Subsidy Armistice." *The Wall Street Journal*.

The United Nations. July 10, 2014. "The World Urbanization Prospect."

The World Service. October 28, 2019. "Abu Bakr al-Baghdadi: IS Leader 'Dead After US Raid' in Syria." *The BBC*.

Thorne, J. March 29, 2011. "Carbon Capture Is All the Rage. Can These Startups Make It Profitable." *PitchBook*.

Tiffany, K. July/August 2021. "The Rise and Fall of an American Tech Giant." *The Atlantic*.

Tilley, A. July 30, 2015. "Light Raises $25 Million to Put a DSLR-Quality Camera on You're Your Next Smartphone." *Forbes*.

Tilley, A. September 14, 2020. "Microsoft Seeks Startup Partnerships in Battle With Amazon Over Cloud." *The Wall Street Journal*.

Tiwary, T. December 09, 2019. "Co-working Company Huddle, GrowX Launch Accelerator for EV Startups." *TechCircle*.

Toplensky, R. November 22, 2021. "A Global Carbon Price Is a Mirage." *The Wall Street Journal*.

Tran, K. October 17, 2017. "Facebook Lets Marketers Analyze User Posts to Guide Ad Strategies." *Business Insider*.

Trentman, N. and M. Maurer. September 14, 2021. "Stock Buybacks Beat Capital Spending for Many Big Companies." *The Wall Street Journal*.

TVA Editors. n.d. "Electric Vehicles." Tennessee Valley Authority. TVA.GOV.

UBS Research Note. 2018. "FLEX: Good time for Entry Plus Optionality From Two Software Assets."

UNCC Editors. n.d. "Home Page." Regional Analytical Chemistry Laboratory. https://rachelab.charlotte.edu

UPS.com Editors. May 26, 2021. "A Century of Smart Business Bets." *United Parcel Service*.

US Space Force Editors. n.d. "Landing Page." Official United States Air Force Website. www.spaceforce.mil

USG. October 12, 2017. "ORNL's New Lab Director Takes a Spin in the 3d Printed Shelby Cobra." *YouTube*.

Vidino, L., J. Lewis, and A. Mines. September 2020. "Dollars for Daesh. Analyzing the Finances of American ISIS Supporters." *The Program on Extremism*. George Washington University.

Vincent, J. May 16, 2019. "Watch and Autonomous Drone Dodge, Duck, Dip, Dive and Dodge a Football." *The Verge*.

Waters, T. May 1997. "Component Branding: Making One Product Indispensable Inside Another." *Innovative Leader* 6, no. 5.

Webb, K. December 11, 2019. "The World's First Electric Commercial Airplane Just Completed a Test Flight." *Business Insider*.

Website Editors. n.d. "Innovation at Lear." *Lear.com*.

Website Editors. n.d. "Our Approach." *Nationwide Ventures*.

Weekly, D. October 23, 2020. "Why Corporate Incubators Fail. And an Idea on What to Do About It." *dweekly (blog)*.

White House Editors. n.d. "Leadership Bio—Megan Smith." Office of Science and Technology Policy. The Obama White House.GOV. https://obamawhitehouse.archives.gov/administration/eop/ostp/about/leadershipstaff/smith (accessed April 03, 2022).

Wiggers, K. July 30, 2018. "One the Eve of a 6 Month Pilot, Drive.AI Details Its Self Driving Car Plans." *Venturebeat*.

Williams, R. October 23, 2017. "Nike's Focus on Robotics Threatens Asia's Low Cost Factories." *The Financial Times*.

Wong, J. January 13, 2017. "Nintendo May Not Know How the Game Is Played." *The Wall Street Journal*.

Wray, S. April 26, 2021. "Berlin Named as Europe's Top City for Startups." *Cities Today*.

Wren, W. September 27, 2019. "This Electrified VW Might Be the Future of Shop Classes." *Autoweek*.

Xcelerator. 2021. Honda Innovations.

Yadron, D. August 25, 2015. "Manager at Video Game Maker Accused of Trade Secret Theft." *The Wall Street Journal*.

About the Author

Tom Waters is an experienced corporate innovator, university mentor, and start-up CEO. He has been a keynote speaker on start-ups and strategy in Silicon Valley, New York, Boston, and London. He is the author of the competitive strategy book *Hyperformance* (Wiley, 2010) and the debut novel *SECRET SIGNS* (Gallaudet University Press, 2011), winner of the International Book Award for Multicultural Fiction.

Tom is the inaugural Assistant Director of start-ups at the University of South Florida, a Tier 1 research institution that is among the top ten in patent creation for public universities, and U.S. News & World Report's fastest rising university of the past decade. There he is taking university IP and creating new start-up companies from Tampa Bay to Biscayne Bay (Miami).

He was previously on the CEO's Corporate Strategy Team at Jabil, leading a team analyzing how innovations in blockchain, augmented reality, A/I, and cybersecurity affected customers such as Apple, GoPro, and Tesla. Tom helped incubate internal start-ups and external acquisitions and was also a mentor for university start-ups working in artificial intelligence, smart municipal bonds, and virtual reality.

He was prior a start-up CEO himself, cofounding Autography LLC with Robert Barrett. Together they received a dozen patents on authentication, biometrics, and digital rewards programs. Autography won the 2011 New York City Digital Show and Tell, and was featured in *The New York Times* and on *ABC's Good Morning America*.

Tom previously worked for SPADAC, a Software-as-a-Service provider of geospatial modeling services to Google Earth and the Department of Defense. Before that he worked in Economics and Trade Security for the Central Intelligence Agency, writing for the President's Daily Brief and informing members of Congress on intellectual property theft by foreign governments. He began his career with a decade in the product development shop at BASF Corporation.

Tom has been interviewed by the *New York Law Journal,* the *Wall Street Journal,* and featured on the cover of *Government Executive Magazine.* He has appeared on *Fox News,* the *BBC,* and RTE Radio Ireland. His nonfiction book *Class 11: Inside the CIA's First Post 9/11 Spy Class* was published by Dutton in 2006 and optioned twice for television by ABC Pictures.

Index

www.ingramcontent.com/pod-product-compliance
Lightning Source LLC
Chambersburg PA
CBHW061309220326
41599CB00026B/4806